Cambridge Elements ≡

Elements in Ancient and Pre-modern Economies
edited by
Kenneth G. Hirth
The Pennsylvania State University
Timothy Earle
Northwestern University
Emily J. Kate
The University of Vienna

SHELL MONEY

A Comparative Study

Mikael Fauvelle
Lund University

Shaftesbury Road, Cambridge CB2 8EA, United Kingdom

One Liberty Plaza, 20th Floor, New York, NY 10006, USA

477 Williamstown Road, Port Melbourne, VIC 3207, Australia

314–321, 3rd Floor, Plot 3, Splendor Forum, Jasola District Centre, New Delhi – 110025, India

103 Penang Road, #05–06/07, Visioncrest Commercial, Singapore 238467

Cambridge University Press is part of Cambridge University Press & Assessment, a department of the University of Cambridge.

We share the University's mission to contribute to society through the pursuit of education, learning and research at the highest international levels of excellence.

www.cambridge.org
Information on this title: www.cambridge.org/9781009494434

DOI: 10.1017/9781009263344

First published 2024

A catalogue record for this publication is available from the British Library.

ISBN 978-1-009-49443-4 Hardback
ISBN 978-1-009-26335-1 Paperback
ISSN 2754-2955 (online)
ISSN 2754-2947 (print)

Shell Money

A Comparative Study

Elements in Ancient and Pre-modern Economies

DOI: 10.1017/9781009263344
First published online: February 2024

Mikael Fauvelle
Lund University
Author for correspondence: Mikael Fauvelle, mikael.fauvelle@ark.lu.se

Abstract: Where, when, and under what circumstances did money first emerge? This Element examines this question through a comparative study of the use of shells to facilitate trade and exchange in ancient societies around the world. It argues that shell money was a form of social technology that expanded political-economic capacities by enabling long-distance trade across boundaries and between strangers. The Element examines several cases in which shells and shell beads permeated throughout daily life and became central to the economic functioning of the societies that used them. In several of these cases, it argues that shells were used in ways that meet all the standard definitions of modern money. By examining the wide range of uses of shell money in ancient economic systems around the world, this Element explores the diversity of forms that money has taken throughout human history. This title is also available as Open Access on Cambridge Core.

Keywords: origins of money, shell beads, trade and exchange, economic anthropology, political economy

ISBNs: 9781009494434 (HB), 9781009263351 (PB), 9781009263344 (OC)
ISSNs: 2754-2955 (online), 2754-2947 (print)

Contents

1 What Is Money?

Even love has not turned more men into fools than has mediation on the nature of money.

William Gladstone, quoted in Marx (1859)

Few things are as central to modern life as money. Nearly every aspect of our daily lives, from the food we eat to the homes we sleep in, is acquired by money. Money is so ubiquitous that it is nearly impossible to imagine life without it. Historically, its tenacity has been so great that even authoritarian attempts to limit or reduce its use, such as in the early days of the Soviet Union or Cambodia's Khmer Rouge, have ended in failure (Figes, 2017; Tyner, 2020). On an international scale, monetary policy holds powerful sway, with organizations such as the US Federal Reserve, the European Central Bank, and the International Monetary Fund able to set interest rates on monetary debts that can make and often break the wealth of nations. For modern society then, it is not an exaggeration to say that "money makes the world go round" (Kander et al., 1966).

But this has not always been the case. Even in the contemporary world, we find examples of people – generally mobile hunters and gatherers such as the Hadza in Africa and Ache in South America – among whom money is rarely used for day-to-day transactions. Rather than money, most such economies are based on debt and reciprocity, with the understanding that goods and services rendered will be rewarded at a later date with similar items or social prestige (Crittenden & Zes, 2015; Stibbard-Hawkes et al., 2022). Expanding our scope to cover all of human history, money is a relatively recent phenomenon that developed at particular places and times. Archaeological finds of physical money – be it metal coins, salt, shell beads, cacao beans, or any of several other forms (see Section 1.3) – generally date to the past several thousand years, as do archaeological indicators of the market-exchange systems that often correlate with monetary economies (Baron & Millhauser, 2021; Feinman & Garraty, 2010). Despite money's ubiquity today, most of the economic systems that have existed in the world have been nonmonetary. These facts pose the following question: Where, when, and under what circumstances did money start being used?

For much of the nineteenth and twentieth centuries, many economists thought they had an answer. Money was seen as one of the hallmarks of civilization, together with such innovations as the political state, urban living, and written communication. In a story advocated by economic theorists ranging from Aristotle to Adam Smith and retold in numerous economics textbooks, monetary exchange is seen as flowing naturally from more simple barter economies

(Begg et al., 2014; see also Graeber, 2011; Stevenson & Wolfers, 2020). Before the development of money, it is argued that exchanges were necessarily based on a coincidence of wants – if you were hungry and without food but had an excess of obsidian blades, you could exchange one of your blades with a successful fisher in need of a new knife. As economies grew and became more complex, it became impractical to constantly search for trading partners who needed the exact goods that one had to offer, leading to the coalescence around certain common and widely desired trade currencies. Precious metals, due to their scarcity and durability, were an obvious choice to fill this need, and goods began to be traded based on their value in weights of copper, silver, or gold (Powell, 1996). When early kings needed to pay armies and sought to control markets, metal (first in weights and later as coins) was used as a currency by the state, leading to the use of metal money as a medium of exchange and the emergence of debt- and credit-based monetary economics as we know them today.

Unfortunately for economics textbooks, this story has major faults. Recently, anthropologists have reemphasized a point long recognized by ethnographers: barter economies rarely exist in the real world. As discussed by David Graeber (2011) and others (Humphrey, 1985; Martin, 2013), most ethnographically known examples of barter-like exchange systems occur during meetings of trading partners from different regions who know that they may never meet again. In communities where every member knows everyone else (basically every village society or hunter-gatherer band), exchanges of goods stemming from the coincidence of wants simply do not take place. Instead, in small-scale societies, exchanges between group members occur within already-established social relationships and come with an expectation of reciprocity. In the previous example, if your neighbor the fisher needs a new obsidian knife and you have a spare, you would likely give one to the fisher even if you were not hungry, knowing that at some point in the future you might need fish, and they would happily share it with you. Such systems of credit and delayed or generalized reciprocity are commonly observed by anthropologists studying nonmonetary economic systems around the world and are likely to have characterized most prestate societies. In other words, money could not have been invented to alleviate burdensome barter economies, since such economies are unlikely to have been present in the ancient world.

There is another major reason why common textbook accounts of the history of money are wrong. Being cast as a characteristic of civilization makes money closely associated with the formation of ancient states. According to the chartalist school of economics first proposed by George Fredrich Knapp (1924), the origins of money were directly tied to the need of early kings to collect taxes, control markets, and pay soldiers (see Rosenswig, 2023 for a contemporary argument for the chartalist approach). Through the backing of a sovereign, the value represented by money became guaranteed, giving stability to its value and facilitating its use to pay debts. Yet descriptions of nonstate monetary systems abound in the ethnographic literature. Throughout the world, an array of objects, ranging from feathers to beans, was used to facilitate exchanges and pay debts in societies ranging from hierarchical chiefdoms to egalitarian bands (Baron & Millhauser, 2021; Earle, 2018; Gamble, 2020). These currencies may not have been controlled by the state but did fulfill many of the other functions commonly attributed to money. Recent calls within archaeology have asked us to cast aside models that place the state at the top of evolutionary typologies and instead envision the variability of experimentation with political organization that seems to have taken place across our history (Graeber & Wengrow, 2021). This Element asks us to do the same for ancient economies by taking seriously the many accounts of Indigenous monetary systems found across the world.

This brings us to shell beads. In the premodern world, shell beads were second only to metal coins in the scale and intensity of their economic use and circulation. On the Pacific coast of North America, millions of diminutive *Olivella* beads were drilled from the thickest portion of the shell and traded across the American West, where many Indigenous cultures used them as a trade currency (Gamble, 2020; Smith & Fauvelle, 2015). In the Indian ocean, cowrie shells from the Maldives were traded across Asia and Africa to the extent that the classical Chinese character for money (貝 *bèi*) represents a stylized cowrie shell (Yang, 2018). Even colonial-era European explorers saw shells as money, carrying millions of them around the world to facilitate exchanges with local peoples. Many anthropological discussions of shell beads, however, have questioned the degree to which these beads functioned as true money, arguing that, in most cases, shell beads circulated within elite political economies without impacting daily transactions (Graeber, 1996, 2001, 2011; cf. Graeber & Wengrow, 2021: 251). The rest of this section forms an overview of approaches to studying shells as money and suggests that recent calls to see money as a form of "social technology" (Felten, 2022; Peneder, 2022) help us to understand the ways that shell currencies were used in ancient economies. Within this framework, the Element compares examples of shell beads from around the world in order to determine where, when, and under what circumstances such beads came to be used as money.

1.1 Functions and Origins of Money

Why do we use money? Since the nineteenth century, economists have generally agreed that money has four functions: a medium of exchange, a measure of value, a standard of deferred payment, and a store of value (Jevons, 1875). Arguably the most important is money's role as a medium of exchange. When we use money to buy groceries, pay for a meal at a restaurant, or collect salaries in return for labor, we exploit money's ability to facilitate exchange in economic systems larger than the household. Although the idea that money developed directly from barter economies has now largely been discredited (Graeber, 2011, see previous section), the ethnographic and archaeological record indicates that many different goods and commodities were used throughout our past as media of exchange, especially in places with heavy and sustained trade across boundaries and between regions (Baron & Millhauser, 2021; Gamble, 2020; Powell, 1996; Smith & Fauvelle, 2015). Some of these commodity-exchange systems took on other functions of money, expanding the economic capacities of the societies that used them within and outside of household and village groups.

Money's function as a measure of value is related to its role as a medium of exchange. If most exchanges are denominated using a specific good or commodity, then evaluations of value will begin to be described in such units as well. Modern people, for example, use dollars, euros, yen, pounds, or other currencies to describe the value of just about anything ranging from time and labor to goods and services. Having standard units to describe wide and varied types of activities greatly facilitates economic exchange and simplifies record-keeping. Units of value need not be exclusive, as many economies use in tandem multiple standards of value. This was also true in the recent past, where coins struck from gold, silver, and other kinds of metals often circulated in the same economic systems.

A most important function of money is as a standard of deferred payment – in other words, its role in the payment of debts. Debts are delayed payments that stem primarily from social arrangements between people rather than goods exchanged or traded. Debts are used to arrange marriages, to pay for losses in gambling, or to settle disputes between aggrieved parties. The collection and payment of debts can be a major purview of the political elite, who often form alliances and solidify power through the giving of gifts that must later be reciprocated. In nonstate societies, shell beads and other commodity monies are often used to denominate such gifts that circulate through elite political-economic systems, possibly making the payment of debts one of the oldest functions of money.

In order for other functions to work, money must be a dependable store of value. In other words, the value of money cannot rapidly increase or decrease. One would not want to incur a debt or conduct long-distance trade using money that might significantly depreciate in value when one's affairs are completed. In modern economic systems, inflation is usually kept in check through the manipulation of interest rates by national banks. Coins held value due to the scarcity of metals used in their manufacture yet could lose value through time due to reduction in weight or debasement through the addition of less valuable metals, sometimes necessitating the introduction of new and more valuable coins. Other forms of money also hold their value through natural scarcity of the materials involved in their manufacture, labor costs associated with production, and removal from circulation during burials and other destructive rituals.

But what about shell money? Most scholars have long recognized that many prestate societies use a range of different goods, often termed as primitive money or commodity money, to fulfill one or more of the above functions. Yet what, if anything, distinguishes cowrie shells, dentalium beads, feather blankets, and other valuables from the dollars and euros that we use today? For most economists, the general consensus is that commodity monies fulfill only a couple of the functions of money, while "true money" fulfills all four (Dalton, 1965). Cowrie shells, for example, might be used during an exchange of bridewealth debt (deferred payment) but not always as a general unit of account. As we have seen previously, however, the different functions of money are largely interrelated. Any good that is used to denominate debts is likely to also function as a unit of account and a store of value. In general, most critiques of commodity valuables as money have fallen into two categories: claims that commodity money was not used in daily transactions and therefore does not fulfill the first function of money (medium of exchange), and arguments that commodity monies were entangled in social relationships and thus did not really function as truly fungible units of account.

David Graeber (1996, 2001, 2011) is one of the most prominent scholars to have argued that the shell beads found in prestate societies around the world should not be considered as true money. According to Graeber, shell beads are closely linked to personal adornment and have been used throughout the world to signify authority and power (Graeber, 1996). When they are exchanged, he argues, shell beads function primarily for social relations such as the arrangement of marriages or the payment of debts, not for everyday purchase of everyday goods. "Primitive currencies of this sort are only rarely used to buy and sell things, and even when they are, never primarily to buy and sell everyday items such as chickens or eggs or shoes or potatoes" (Graeber, 2011: 60). Yet these are modern examples of exchanges, and, as Graeber himself often notes, ancient economies did not really work this way. In most prestate societies, household production provided most people with food, clothes, and other items used in day-to-day lives. When goods did change hands, it was often under the purview of the elite political economy – precisely the place where we see shell-bead wealth being exchanged.

Stating that shell beads cannot have been money since they did not facilitate ordinary economic exchanges places the onus on the anthropologist to determine what such an economy should have looked like. Often, the everyday exchanges described – shoes, eggs, chickens, and the like – closely mirror things that are bought and sold in modern market economies. This sets up a circular argument where ancient and nonstate money is not seen as "true money" if it is not used for the types of interactions that modern money is used for. If we expand our concept of the "ordinary" economy to focus on the types of exchanges that ancient people were more likely to make, we might see that items such as shell beads did indeed grease the wheels of a majority of economic interactions. A more emic approach to understanding ancient economies, therefore, might find that shell or other commodity money was just as central to economic activity as modern money is to our lives today.

An argument similar to Graeber's against the use of money in prestate societies has recently been made by Rosenswig (2023), based on archaeological case studies drawn largely from ancient Mesoamerica. Embracing a chartalist position, Rosenswig defines money as "a system of accounting" and argues that it arose from the need for ancient states to collect taxes and tribute. He briefly discusses "non-state" money yet follows Graeber by arguing that such monies worked as "social accounting systems" rather than "financial accounting systems" and thus cannot be classified as true money. Leaving aside the fact that modern money also functions as a system of social accounting (see Section 1.2), this argument is prone to the same circular logic. By defining money based on its function as a unit of account, Rosenswig deemphasizes other functions of money that might be more readily observable in nonstate societies. Although ancient states needed money to function as a unit of account for the purposes of tax collection, this does exclude the use of money for other functions (for example, as a medium of exchange) in prestate societies.

Another common argument against characterizing shell beads as money is that they are socially embedded (Dalton, 1965; Gregory, 1982). True money, it is argued, is alienable and asocial. One ten-euro note is the same as any other and is of equal value regardless of who holds it. Many forms of ancient money, however, derived value in part from their own history of exchange. Certain strands of shell beads that were traded between powerful chiefs or at important feasts may be seen as more valuable than others, calling into question their fungibility. On closer scrutiny, however, we can see that modern money can also work in similar ways. Much as shell beads circulated within the prestige economies of chiefly feasts, the world of modern finance is well known to be lubricated by expensive gifts, elaborate dinners, political connections, and other forms of social connections. In less elite situations, modern money is also socially embedded, being transferred through inheritance and weddings and given as birthday presents, waiter's tips, and children's allowances (Zelizer, 2021). We even distinguish between "dirty money" and "honest money," showing that item histories still pertain to modern currency (Brück, 2015; Zelizer, 2021). To say that shell money cannot be compared to modern money due to its socially embedded nature is thus a strawman argument comparing ancient money to an imagined modern ideal that does not conform to lived experience.

These critiques, that prestate money was not "true money" because it was not used for daily exchanges and was often embedded in social relationships, stem largely from using modern money as a starting point for comparison. If we set out to find an exact analog to modern money in the past, then we are unlikely to find many matching case studies. Such a strategy, however, glosses over the great variety of complex economic formations that have existed around the world and throughout history. A more inclusive approach to money illustrates deep and long-lasting traditions of using various items to facilitate trade and pay debts, especially in locations with regular and sustained interregional trade and travel. Such an approach can also account for the multitude of different, unconventional ways in which money is also used in modern settings, which is why many contemporary economists have started to adopt a more social understanding of what money is (Felten, 2022; Ingham, 1996; Zelizer, 2021). In this Element, I draw from several contemporary economists to envision money as a social technology that enables, facilitates, and expands a society's economic capacity.

1.2 Money as Social Technology

Most orthodox approaches to money see it as objective and individualist, working in the background of modern economies to facilitate exchange, manage accounts, demark debts, and store value. Several heterodox economists, however, have long emphasized the profoundly social, situational, and innovative capacities of money to expand human economic systems (Peneder, 2022). Joseph Schumpeter, for example, wrote that "the function of money in the economy is in principle of a merely technical nature, i.e. money is essentially a device for carrying on business transactions" (Schumpeter, 1917, quoted in Peneder, 2022: 180). The connection between technology and money has perhaps never before been as evident as today, with the current proliferation of experimentation with different digital and cryptocurrencies (Peneder, 2022).

Diverse social payments, however, are just as common in the "real" economy as they are in cyberspace. As discussed by Zelizer (2000; 2021), money in modern society can take many different forms, circulating as gambling chips, lunch tickets, gift certificates, airline miles, and a plethora of other media that exist alongside state-issued currency. These social monies are not so different from the many different trade currencies that have existed throughout human history, showing that humans have long experimented with different forms of exchange in order to solve the economic problems that face them.

An excellent case study into the plural forms that money can take is Felten's (2022) analysis of church finance in the early modern Dutch Republic. Discussing the efforts of a seventeenth-century parish community to build a new church near the border town of Bredevoort, he describes how parish officials raised funds in various forms to support constructing a new church. Parishioners paid with grains, wood, tobacco, or labor, each contribution being carefully tabulated by the church. Even equal contributions demarcated in metal coins were valued differently based on the positions of the individuals who donated them. Felten (2022: 26) argues that through raising funds to build their church, the parishioners of Bredevoort gave meaning and value both to different money-objects as well as to the people exchanging them. Drawing from Francesca Bray's (1999: 166) discussion of technology as something that has the ability to impart meaning, contains energy, and reproduces social structures, Felten suggests that money should be seen as a social technology that connects people, money, meaning, and value. Any object could be considered as money so long as it was exchangeable across both time and social divides. The question, then, is understanding how the relationships between people and money are created and maintained.

The term "social technology" is used to describe internet applications such as social media or digital conferencing (Peneder, 2022). Building on Felten (2022), I see social technology as broadly encompassing all material and nonmaterial innovations that expand the capacity of human societies to build meaningful connections between people. Examples of social technology include concepts such as writing, legal codes, mathematics, or the Internet, all of which had wide-reaching effects on the societies that developed them. Social technology might be associated with a suite of material artifacts – for example, clay tablets and reed styluses in the case of Mesopotamian writing – but exists independently from such artifacts as a social phenomenon. As such, social technology exists somewhere between the "techniques" and "sociotechnical systems" described by Pfaffeberger (1992) as different levels of technology. Unlike the wheel, the plow, or other critical material-technological innovations, money takes many different forms yet provides the same important functions and capacities to the societies that have developed it. As social technology, money provided societies with enhanced capacities to engage in economic functions such as long-distance trade or the accumulation of wealth, providing opportunities that would not have been possible without its use.

Graeber (2012) has invoked similar terminology when discussing shell beads as a form of social currency. While arguing that shell beads cannot be money due to their perceived lack of integration into daily exchange, he nonetheless acknowledges the critical importance that shell-bead exchange has had in many cultures around the world (Graeber, 1996, 2012). In order to account for this, he argues that shell beads work as a form of social currency, distinguished from money in that they work primarily to transform social relationships rather than to further the exchange of material goods (Graeber, 2012: 412). Setting aside the fact that many shell beads did facilitate material exchange, I agree that strengthening social bonds was central for many shell-bead economies the world over. I do not, however, agree that this makes shell beads any less money-like, especially considering that many of the social functions that Graeber ascribes to social currency are equally important for our money today. Instead of dividing up different kinds of currency and debating which are really money, I prefer to approach money as a continuum, with many different currencies having been developed at different points in time in response to various economic needs.

The concept of social technology also has parallels with Goody's (1977) idea of a "technology of the intellect" and Mann's (1986) discussion of infrastructural power. For Goody, technology of the intellect referred primarily to writing and literacy, which he saw as expanding both the cognitive and organizational capacities of ancient societies in radical new ways. In a similar vein, Mann focused on how universalizing technologies such as literacy, markets, and coinage allowed for larger and more integrated formulations of power. For both scholars, these technologies were key to the underpinnings of early states, as they enabled larger and more expansive state apparatuses to form. In this Element, I use social technology as a broader term for any concept or technique that can be used to build and enable communications and interactions between groups. In other words, social technologies enhance the abilities of groups to build and maintain social ties. Money fills this role as it facilitates connections between people. This was especially true for many of the examples of shell money described in this Element, which were often traded in cases of intense interregional exchange. Social technology can enhance regional integration in ways that facilitate the formation of ancient states but can also provide economic benefits to nonstate societies and actors. As I argue throughout this

Element, money fits this role well, as it was widely used by prestate societies yet also proved highly conducive to eventual state formation.

I present money as a social technology that, in the words of sociologist Geoffrey Ingham, "expands human society's capacity to get things done" (2013: 4). As such, money can perform different functions with varying emphases, at different times, in different societies, and in different contexts. In the vast trading spheres of oceanic Asia and inland North America, for example, cowrie and *Olivella* shells played critical roles in facilitating trade between many cultures and peoples. In the woodlands of eastern North America, on the other hand, wampum was exchanged during alliance feasts and weddings, mediating social ties between both individuals and groups. That money might have a continuum of uses is not exclusive to the premodern world, as can be seen from the wide range of forms and functions of modern money from stock dividends to meal vouchers (Zelizer, 2000). By investigating different case studies across time and space, we search for commonalities in the material characteristics of different forms of money that allowed its functions to be performed in order to address the central question of where, when, and in what circumstances money started to be used.

1.3 Grounds for Comparison: What Makes Something Money?

Seeing money as a continuum, how can we identify its past use? Considering the four classical functions of money, any item used as money needs to have properties that facilitate these different roles. On a basic level, money must be storable, countable, and transferable, meaning that money-items need to be durable, transportable, and relatively standardized. To facilitate exchanges across wide regions, it should be held in comparable value across social boundaries. In order to work as either a medium of exchange or a standard of deferred payment, money must also be a store of value, which means there must be some mechanism by which money can counteract the effects of inflation. Finally, money must be able to expand the economic possibilities of the people who use it, meaning that it must be widely acceptable and socially valued. These different characteristics all point to material correlates that can be used to evaluate the degree to which circulating commodities may or may not have functioned as money.

One of the most basic attributes of money is its ability to be transported, counted, and exchanged in broad personal networks. Although this trait is most closely connected to money's role as a medium of exchange, it is also important for paying debts and other functions that transfer value. The easiest way to ensure that money works in this capacity is for money-items to be made from durable and storable materials that can be easily handled and are unlikely to be damaged in transport. Metal excels at this (both as a weighed currency and as coinage), as do small and hard items such as shell beads or cacao beans. Not all examples of ancient monies fit the above criteria. Salt bars, for example, were a form of currency used in ancient Ethiopia, yet they were notoriously brittle and vulnerable to destruction by moisture (Felten, 2022). These characteristics, however, ensured that many damaged bars left circulation and worked to reduce inflation.

All money systems must have restraints to limit inflation if they are to function as a store of value. This issue is commonly raised by economists discussing shell beads, who argue that if anyone could collect shells from the beach and use them for money, it would not be long until inflation made shells worthless. Shell-money systems generally avoided this problem in two different ways. One was through the difficulty of manufacturing many small beads. If labor costs were high and specialized skills were required for production, the supply of shell beads entering an exchange system would be sufficiently limited to keep exchange values steady. In other case studies, shells acted as money in regions far removed from the oceans where they were collected, keeping inflation in check through the difficulties of transport. In both cases, shell beads were generally removed from circulation through burials and caching, taking money out of circulation and further reducing inflation.

Another highly desirable characteristic for money is that each exchange item be of equal value to all the others. In other words, money needs to be mutually exchangeable (fungible). Although not all valuables on the money continuum fit this criterion (see Section 2), it is a common characteristic for all unambiguous examples of exchange money. Fungibility is usually achieved through standardization in weight or size (Earle, 2018). Shell-bead money and minted coins, for example, are usually produced to exacting standards of uniformity, while cacao beans and cowrie shells are naturally uniform in shape. A standardized series of weights, such as those used in ancient Mesopotamia, can also achieve uniformity for a metal-based currency system (Powell, 1996). Fungibility is especially important for money that is used in long-distance trade where the parties involved might not fully trust or know their exchange partners. Standardization of production is also a characteristic that is thankfully easy to identify by an analysis of archaeological materials.

Although many different items fit the above criteria and have been used as money by cultures around the world, this Element focuses on shells. This is because shells are one of the oldest, most common, and most widespread forms of money to have been used across human history. I focus on discussing several different case studies of shell and shell-bead exchange (Figure 1). Following the

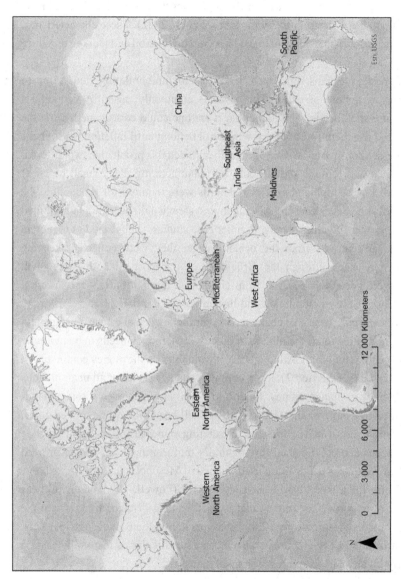

Figure 1 Map showing world regions discussed in book. Map by Mikael Fauvelle

idea that we can see money as a continuum, these case studies will be loosely organized in a sequence from those where the "money-ness" of circulated shells is somewhat ambiguous to those where shells and shell beads were widely described and used as money by all parties involved in their exchange. Through these case studies, I highlight the attributes and functions of money described above to evaluate the degree to which shell beads in each case were used as money and address the overarching question of where, when, and under what circumstances the powerful phenomenon we call money first started to shape human societies.

2 The Mediterranean, Europe, and the South Pacific

If a person is seeking a kitomwa [shell wealth] *then first he must feed his pig. He feeds the pig, he feeds it and it grows big. Then a man comes along, he wants a pig. He pays the price set by the man who reared the pig. If he wants bagi* [shell necklaces], *then bagi, if mwali* [shell armbands], *then mwali. It's up to the owner to set the terms.*

Tubetube islander discussing the sale of a pig for shell wealth.
Quoted in Macintyre (1983a: 126)

This section begins our comparison with several case studies of shells and shell wealth that are not traditionally treated as money in the archaeological and anthropological literature. We start with a brief discussion of the antiquity of shell beads in North Africa and the Mediterranean, establishing that humans have long experimented with crafting and trading shell objects. We then turn to two famous cases of shell-bead production and exchange: *Spondylus* shell exchange in Neolithic Europe and the trade of Kula valuables in the South Pacific. In both cases, shell beads crossed cultural boundaries and expanded the economic capacity of the societies that used them. While the limitation of the archaeological record makes it difficult to determine exactly how *Spondylus* shells were used, I suggest that strings of shells known as *Kitomwa* functioned for a range of ceremonial and more mundane uses, closely approximating the functions of shell money discussed in the previous section. These examples point to the antiquity and diversity of different experimentations with the money-like exchange of shell valuables in different parts of the world.

2.1 Antiquity of Shell Beads

Shell beads are one of the oldest and most widespread forms of symbolic technology in human history. The use of shell beads is a trait that we share with our nearest ancestors, the Neanderthals, who produced perforated and painted marine shell beads over 115,000 years ago in southern Spain

(Hoffmann et al., 2018). The earliest evidence of shell-bead production by anatomically modern humans dates to around the same time or shortly thereafter, with perforated shells found at the Es Skhul cave site in Israel and the Blombos Cave in southern Africa (Figure 2), both dated to around 100,000

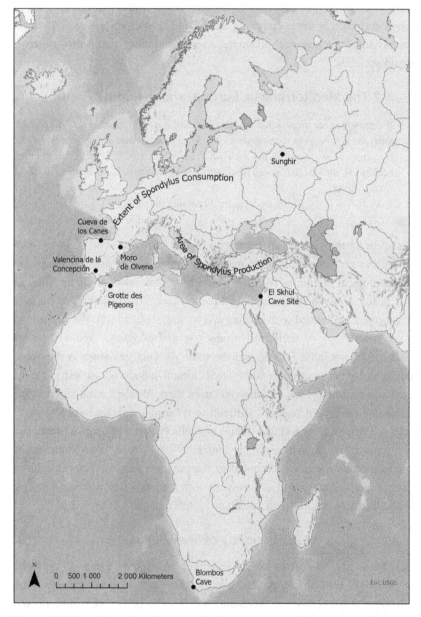

Figure 2 Map of locations discussed in Sections 2.1 and 2.2. Map by Mikael Fauvelle

years ago (d'Errico et al., 2005; Vanhaeren et al., 2006). Even during the Middle Paleolithic, shell beads were traded far and wide, likely owing to their durability and portability. In Africa, starting as early as 50,000 years ago, drilled and shaped beads made from ostrich shells share stylistic and metric similarities across both southern and eastern Africa (Miller & Wang, 2021), strongly suggesting that beads were traded between these two areas. Although it is unlikely that these early beads functioned as money, the production and exchange of shell beads has been an important part of human economic activity for most of our history.

Why did our early ancestors start making shell beads? The contexts and conditions in which these earliest beads have been found offer a clue. In both the Es Skhul and Blombos caves, red ochre was found, including directly on four *Glycymeris* sp. shells in the Blombos cave (d'Errico et al., 2005; Vanhaeren et al., 2006). At another Middle Paleolithic cave site located in modern-day Morocco, nine perforated *Tritia gibbosula* shells were also found with red ochre residues (Bouzouggar et al., 2007). In many of these cases, use-wear patterns on the beads suggest that they were strung through their perforations, a practice that may have been shared with Neanderthals (Hardy et al., 2020). The decoration of beads with bright red colors suggests that they were meant for display and likely functioned as personal adornment worn either on clothes or separately as a necklace or bracelet. Such decorations likely served as markers of social identity, signifying the status of the wearer either within their own social group or in comparison with different groups (d'Errico & Vanhaeren, 2015). The labor involved in making the beads, together with the distance that would have been traveled to acquire them, would have marked the status of those who wore them.

The use of shell beads as items of personal adornment is hardly unique to the Middle Paleolithic. Nearly all cases described in this Element include examples of worn shell beads, highlighting the close association between the accumulation of wealth and the desire to signify social status. The practice of wearing one's wealth is just as common today as it was in the past, as can be seen in both high-end fashion and expensive jewelry. The act of incorporating money into clothing has both modern and historical parallels (Figure 3). Of course, the fuzzy line between money, jewelry, and status display makes it hard to identify money in the archaeological record. While everyone might agree that designer clothing signifies wealth and status, no one would argue that this makes it money. To fulfill its four functions, money must instead have physical characteristics that facilitate exchange. With respect to shell beads, this means they must be both durable and highly standardized. In this sense, beads covered in red ochre likely were more for display than exchange.

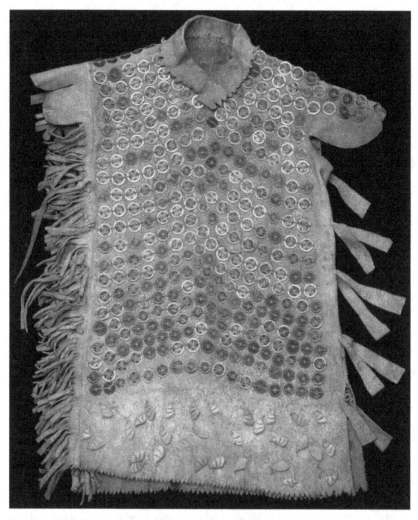

Figure 3 Tlingit armor incorporating Chinese coins, mid-19th century. Museum Purchase, 1869. Courtesy of the Peabody Museum of Archaeology and Ethnology, Harvard University, 69-30-10/2065

We would also expect to find more money-like beads in contexts other than burials or garments, although large amounts of money can also be deposited with the dead (see Sections 3 and 4).

Why were shells traded? In some cases, people seem to have associated shells with water and acquired shell artifacts in order to gain power over rain or other aquatic resources. The massive hoard of over 3.8 million marine shells found at the site of Paquime in the Chihuahuan desert of Mexico has been interpreted as being linked to supernatural power associated with watery themes such as rain and fertility (Whalen, 2013). In inland regions, shells may also have had value due to their relative scarcity and use as a medium for art. The white color and durable nature of shells made them well suited for carving and coloring to make distinctive jewelry and adornment. Although many of them were made from ivory, the over 13,000 beads (including hundreds in shell) found in burials at the Sunghir site in Russia point to the ritual and symbolic importance of beads by at least 30,000 BP (Trinkaus & Buzhilova, 2018). Trading shells is likely to have helped establish and cement bonds both within and between social groups. Being highly portable, shells would have been easy to exchange over large distances and could have been carried by travelers from coastal regions.

Of course, not all cases of shell-bead exchange constitute monetary transactions. In the absence of ethnographic records or historic texts, the exact function of shell beads found in the archaeological record is often unclear. Given that many historical examples of shell-bead use (for example the *Olivella* and cowrie shells presented in Sections 3 and 4) did function as money, we should not rule out the possibility that early shell beads may have had money-like characteristics. As discussed in Section 1, beads that are standardized and regularly exchanged within and between economic systems may have performed some functions of money. With these characteristics in mind, the following section presents famous examples of shell beads that are not widely accepted as having been money but were still central to the political-economic systems of the societies that used them.

2.2 Shell-Bead Exchange and the Origins of European Trade Networks

Europe has a long tradition of producing and trading shell beads, starting during the Paleolithic and continuing into the Mesolithic, Neolithic, and Bronze Ages. Perforated marine snails from the species *Columbella rustica* and *Trivia* sp. are common at Mesolithic sites on the Mediterranean and Atlantic coasts of Europe and are also found at considerable distances inland, especially along river valleys reaching as far as southern Germany (Álvarez Fernandez, 2010). In Spain, perforated shells increase in frequency compared to unperforated beads with distance from the sea, suggesting that beads were produced near the coast and then traded further inland (Álvarez Fernandez, 2010). Most of these beads consist of intact shells perforated either near the base or at the spire point, implying that they were meant to be strung and worn as jewelry. A Late Mesolithic burial at Cueva de Los Canes in northern Spain, for example, found dozens of *Trivia* beads arranged around an individual's neck, upper body, and feet, as if worn as necklaces and foot bracelets (Arias, 2002). These nonstandardized and display-oriented beads suggest that they were unlikely to have been intended to serve as a medium of exchange, yet their wide distribution demonstrates that their trade and use were important social and economic activities for Mesolithic hunter-gatherers.

More standardized disk beads started to be produced during the early Neolithic period, especially in Iberia. Most of these beads were made from cockle shells (*Cardiidae* sp.) by grinding, polishing, and drilling fragmented shells (Álvarez Fernandez, 2010; Benito, 2005). Compared to the spire-lopped and basally perforated snail-shell beads that predominated in earlier periods, these beads required substantially more labor to produce. Neolithic disk beads also display significantly greater uniformity. At the middle Neolithic cave site of Moro de Olvena located in northern Aragón around 180 km from the sea, a total of 118 cockle-shell disk beads clustered into two distinct groups of 1.15 ± .05 cm and 0.85 ± .05 cm (Alday, 1995). Tight clustering suggests standardization in production but could also be explained if the beads were transported to the site in two different items of adornment. Limited finds from the early Neolithic make it difficult to draw generalized conclusions regarding the economic function of cockle disk beads.

Exchange of shells increased drastically during the Late Neolithic, when items made from *Spondylus* shell became among the most widely traded goods in much of Europe (Müller, 1997; Rahmstorf, 2016; Séfériadès, 2010; Windler, 2013, 2019). *Spondylus* is a genus of bivalve mollusks living in warm and tropical waters around the world. In Europe, *S. gaederopus* lives only in the warm waters of the Mediterranean and in prehistory was primarily collected in the Aegean and Adriatic seas. The thick and durable shells of *Spondylus* are perfect for carving beads, bracelets, and other items of art (Figure 4). The best shells for carving must be collected from the live animal, which lives at depths

Figure 4 *Spondylus gaederopus* shell from Spain. Public domain photo from Wikimedia Commons

of 2 to 30 meters, meaning that they were likely collected by diving. Although *Spondylus* can be consumed as food and appears in the archaeological record during the Paleolithic, it was during the Neolithic that the shell was harvested in great quantities, worked into beads and other goods, and traded far and wide across the European continent.

The most intensive period of *Spondylus* shell exchange in Europe seems to have occurred during the second half of the sixth millennium BCE (Windler, 2013, 2019). During this period, shells were collected and worked on the islands and coasts of the Aegean and traded across the continent, reaching dozens of sites as far afield as northern Germany, Poland, and the Paris Basin, where thousands of *Spondylus* artifacts have been found in burials. The dispersal of *Spondylus* shells across Europe coincides with the spread of the Linear Pottery culture and associated Neolithic and agricultural practices across much of Europe. *Spondylus* is the most common material item to have moved across the neolithicized parts of the continent during this time and can be seen as a precursor to later trade routes used during the early Bronze Age (Séfériadès, 2010; Windler, 2019). Traded items made from *Spondylus* include many thousands of cylinder beads, bracelets, and clasps, as well as more unique items of art such as small animal effigies.

Why did Neolithic Europeans exchange *Spondylus* shells across the continent? Most answers have focused on the role of *Spondylus* shells and jewelry as items of wealth and prestige (Müller, 1997; Windler, 2013). The fact that *Spondylus* shells are often found in high-status burials, together with other rare and prestigious items such as mace heads, marbles, and imported obsidian, gives testament to its high status and value. Others have suggested that shell artifacts may have been important sources of shamanic power, and that *Spondylus* bracelets and other jewelry may have been handed down through generations as part of shamanic toolkits (Séfériadès, 2010). The idea that *Spondylus* shells from the Mediterranean might have held "superstitious power" in northern Europe goes back to the days of Gordon V. Childe (Séfériadès, 2010: 187) and is reminiscent of the idea that marine shells in the Chihuahuan desert of North America might have held symbolic power associated with water and fertility (Whalen, 2013). They also would likely have held additional prestige due to the great distances over which they were transported and the knowledge of distant places that their ownership might have entailed (Helms, 1993). In addition to their symbolic value, it is clear that *Spondylus* would have had considerable material worth, considering both the great distances involved in their trade as well as the labor needed to collect and carve elaborate jewelry.

One answer to the question of how *Spondylus* shells were used during the Neolithic might come from the substantial regional difference in where the shells were deposited (Figure 2). Across Europe, *Spondylus* shells have been found in many contexts, including hoards, settlements, and burials (Windler, 2013, 2019). In northern Europe, however, finds in burial contexts predominate, while shell finds in domestic contexts are much more common in southeastern Europe and Greece (Müller, 1997; Windler, 2013, 2019). This strongly suggests that the use of *Spondylus* shells may have shifted with distance from their point of origin, with their natural scarcity in northern Europe increasing their value as items of wealth and status. *Spondylus* jewelry might have been more commonly used as an item for display in southeastern Europe, for example, while in the north the shells may have been closely kept as important markers of wealth and value in political-economic exchange systems.

Long-distance trade of *Spondylus* shells decreased toward the end of the Neolithic, with an increased emphasis on exchange in bronze and copper goods. In some regions, however, the use and production of shell beads exploded during the Chalcolithic. In southern Spain, for example, millions of shell beads have been excavated from the Montelirio section of the Valencina de la Concepcion site near Seville, Spain (Diaz-Guardamino Uribe et al., 2016; García Sanjuán et al., 2018). These beads were carved from bivalves and were highly standardized, ranging between 4 and 5 mm in diameter. They are also found by the tens of thousands at adjacent contemporary sites in southern Iberia, although the largest quantities by far come from the elite female burials at Valencina de la Concepción (Diaz-Guardamino Uribe et al., 2016). Unlike neolithic *Spondylus* shells, however, most of these beads are found in burial contexts, are often local, and were mostly worn as adornment. As we shall see in future case studies (see Section 3), this does not preclude their use as money. More examples from domestic contexts, however, would be helpful in building the case for money-like usage. Hopefully future work will shed more light on this intensive Copper Age shell-bead industry.

Were *Spondylus* shells in Europe a form of Neolithic money? Returning to the attributes of money raised in Section 1, the fact that many *Spondylus* beads are deposited in graves would have provided a means to control inflation, as would the fact that in northern Europe they are found over 1,000 kilometers from their point of initial manufacture. To travel this distance, they would certainly have had to cross dozens or even hundreds of political and cultural boundaries and would have been a useful form of portable wealth for conducting trade between strangers. In addition to burials, many *Spondylus* shells are also found in cached hoards, which further suggests that they were seen as a form of wealth to be securely stored and saved (Windler, 2013, 2019). The practice of hoarding shell wealth parallels later hoards of bronze ingots and other items that have been interpreted as trade currencies used during later periods (Vandkilde, 2016).

The presence of *Spondylus* in children's burials (for example, at Durankulak in Bulgaria) also points to their use as a marker of wealth and ascribed status (Windler, 2013: 103). On the other hand, differences in sizes of beads and types of artifacts suggests that Neolithic *Spondylus* shells were not easily interchangeable, suggesting low fungibility that made it unlikely to serve as a standard of payment. In this sense, they may be more comparable to other famous examples of shell valuable exchange such as the Kula ring in the South Pacific, where shells were central to regional political economies but were often highly individual and unique items of wealth and prestige.

2.3 The Kula Ring and the South Pacific

The most famous case of shell-bead exchange is almost certainly the Kula ring, including the Trobriand Islands, located in the South Pacific off the east coast of New Guinea (Figure 5). The Kula ring became one of the canons of anthropological literature due to the work of Bronisław Malinowski, who conducted fieldwork on the islands between 1915 and 1918. During the time of Malinowski and other twentieth-century anthropologists, inhabitants of the Trobriand Islands lived in villages of up to 100 individuals, who raised pigs, cultivated yams, and fished in the sea. They were politically organized into clusters of villages led by individuals who often inherited status, but who

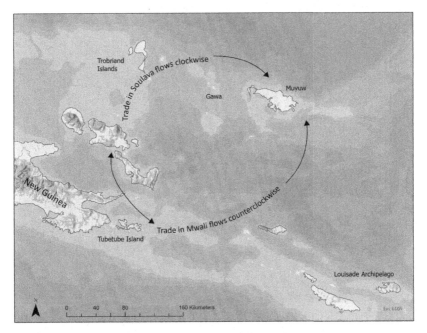

Figure 5 Map of Trobriand Islands and Kula ring. Map by Mikael Fauvelle

nonetheless needed to maintain their positions through status display and competition for followers (Powell, 1960). Because of their long-distance inter-island voyages, Malinowski was fascinated by the maritime exchange system of the Trobriand islanders, famously described as *Argonauts of the Pacific* (Malinowski, 1922). Among the most common items traded on these maritime voyages were shell beads and bracelets.

High-value goods traded between islands to the Trobriands were known as *veguwa* (spelled *vaygua* by Malinowski) (Figure 6). The most famous forms of *veguwa* were shell-disk bead necklaces called *soulava*, and *Conus* shell armbands known as *mwali* (Malinowski, 1921, 1922). These forms of shell wealth were often traded in tandem with each other, so that a trading event that was initiated with the giving of *soulava* would be reciprocated and often terminated with the giving of *mwali*, or vice versa. This system was facilitated by the opposite flow of these goods, with *soulava* being traded in a clockwise direction around the Trobriand archipelago while *mwali* was traded counterclockwise. This linked and reciprocal circular exchange between *soulava* and *mwali* is what Malinowski called the Kula ring. Notably, individual *soulava* necklaces and *mwali* bracelets would accrue prestige as they circulated in this network, with the most prestigious items deriving their value in part from the list of

Figure 6 Kula valuables. *Mwali* armband on the left and *soulava* necklace on the right. © The Trustees of the British Museum

previous owners that would be recited when they were traded. Acquiring powerful *veguwa* and adding their own names to the list of owners was one of the primary ways in which high-status Trobriand men would seek to expand their fame through both space and time and cement their political standing.

Soulava and *mwali* were also not the only shell valuables exchanged on the Trobriands. Strings of *Spondylus* shell disk beads, called *katudababile*, were more standardized in shape than those on *soulava* necklaces and were also traded widely within the archipelago (see Figure 7). Malinowski (1922: 358) emphasizes that *katudababile* did not complete the Kula ring, as they were not traded in a specific direction or in tandem with other values. Additionally, they were not used for powerful spells or other rituals in the same way that more

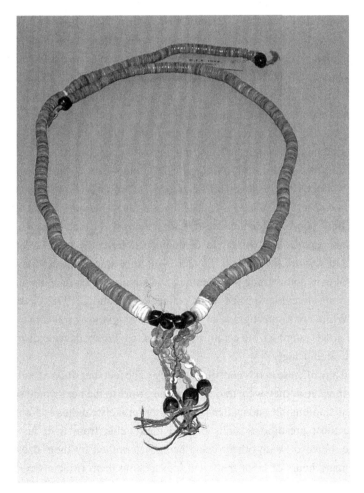

Figure 7 *Katudababile* necklace. © The Trustees of the British Museum

valuable and unique *soulava* and *mwali* were. Nonetheless, from Malinowski's own accounts, *katudababile* shell valuables were important for many economic transactions. For example, he writes how necklaces of *Spondylus* beads were commonly traded for food (1922: 373) and were important components of both bride wealth and chiefly tribute (Brunton, 1975; Malinowski, 1935). Use of *Spondylus* shell disk beads can be° found as exchange goods throughout Micronesia and Melanesia (Macintyre, 1983b: 85; Szabó, 2018). Between *soulava*, *mwali*, and *katudababile*, considerable shell wealth was circulating among the political economic systems of the South Pacific islands during the early twentieth century.

As more fieldwork was conducted on the Trobriands over the course of the twentieth century, views of Kula exchange and Kula valuables expanded beyond the classic image painted by Malinowski and reproduced in most early anthropology textbooks. Research by Weiner (1976) showed that the Kula ring was not just about chiefly men trading high-status *soulava* and *mwali* but also involved exchanges of banana-leaf bundles and skirts made by women and used during important mortuary ceremonies. Other goods exchanged in parallel to the Kula cycle included stone axe heads, clay pots, boar's tusks, canoes, and strings of smaller shell beads not formally classified as *soulava* (Austen, 1945; Earle, 2018; Malinowski, 1922; Weiner, 1976). Food was also exchanged through the Kula ring, including pigs, yams, fish, and other forms of surplus (Austen, 1945; Weiner, 1976). Interisland voyages carried out by traders on the Kula cycle, therefore, transported ritual and prestigious items such as *mwali* and *soulava*, as well as a wide range of more utilitarian and fungible trade goods. Trade in these utilitarian items was called *gimwali*, which Malinowski glossed as "barter" to distinguish it from the more ceremonial exchange of *veguwa* (Malinowski, 1922: 190). Subsequent scholars have suggested that commodity trade was common and almost always accompanied the exchange of more high-profile Kula valuables (Damon, 1978; Macintyre, 1983a). While not as prestigious as Kula exchange, *gimwali* was a major way in which goods ranging from ceramic pots to *Spondylus* shells were distributed across the archipelago.

But did any of these goods constitute money? The fact that *soulava* and *mwali* increase in value as they were traded from one owner to the next would seem to make them nonfungible and inalienable and thus unlikely candidates for money. Only the most prestigious shells derived their value from their history of exchange, however, with others value being determined by their size, color, and the many hours of labor that went into making them (Macintyre, 1983a: 112–115). Maintaining a history of transactions should also not exclude an item from functioning as money, since such transaction histories are central to the functioning of modern cryptocurrencies such as bitcoin. The fact that a hierarchy of shell *veguwa* existed with names for the different ranks (Macintyre, 1983a: 112), implies that these items could be used as trade goods with well-known exchange rates. Recent reevaluations of the economic role of Kula valuables have deemphasized their inalienability and highlighted the ways in which they could be used to achieve economic and political ends (Keesing, 1990). Based on fieldwork on the Trobriand island of Vakuta, for example, Campbell (1983: 204) writes that "it is quite clear that shell valuables can be fed into the internal exchange system as wealth items, thereby securing other wealth in the form of yams, magic, land and women." Based on their fieldwork, Macintyre and Young (1982: 214) also write that "the purpose of Kula is to forge alliances through a sequence of indebtedness and to accumulate valuables which can be used for internal exchange." Clearly Kula has an economic function in addition to the ceremonial roles described by Malinowski.

Exchanges that could be facilitated by shell valuables are described in detail by Macintyre based on her work on the island of Tubetube, located immediately south of the Trobriands (Macintyre, 1983a, 1983b; Macintyre & Young, 1982). Although Tubetube is not part of the Trobriand archipelago, it does take part in Kula exchanges, which are called *Kune* in the local language of Bwanabwana (Macintyre, 1983a: 4). She spent several years conducting ethnographic field-work on Tubetube in the 1970s and 1980s, meticulously documenting the island's political economies (Macintyre, 1983a, 1983b). Shell valuables – including *soulava*, *mwali*, and also red *Spondylus* shells similar to *katudaba-bile* – were exchanged in a wide variety of economic situations. They were given at funerals to the families of the deceased, used to purchase pigs, traded for food including yams and fish, used to pay debts incurred due to lost labor, paid as a form of wealth inheritance to younger generations of a family, used to purchase steel axes, used as payment in land transactions, used to purchase canoes or pay for their construction, used to pay debts incurred by homicide, and used for payment for a range of other services including sorcery (Macintyre, 1983a: 52, 65, 93, 99, 116, 126, 162). Indeed, just about any major transaction a Tubetube islander might want to make could be paid for with shell valuables. On Tubetube, at least, shell valuables seem to have been a central lubricant to economic activities.

Considering the many economic activities paid for with shell valuables, their function in both the payments of debts and the purchase of goods, and their use as a long-term store of value and prestige, did the shell valuables including *soulava*, *mwali*, and *katudababile* (collectively known as *kitomwa*) function as money? Macintyre writes that "*kitomwa* are unequivocally a medium of exchange", elaborating that they also functioned as a store of wealth and unit of account (Macintyre, 1983a: 123–125). Her fieldwork on Tubetube is corroborated by similar findings on Vakuta, where shells also were exchanged for a wide range of goods and services (Campbell, 1983). The money-like attributes of shell valuables were not lost on the Bwanabwana people themselves, who described shells as "Paupuan money" in comparison to "European money" (Macintyre, 1983a: 125). The fact that shell valuables were exchanged for both high-value goods such as pigs and canoes as well as more utilitarian items such as steel tools and fish seems to pass Graeber's test (see Section 1) for money being used for daily transactions. *Kitomwa* also expanded the capacity of Kula traders to conduct economic activities, allowing for the pooling of resources to pay for high-value items such as pigs or canoes. Although *kitomwa* clearly has important ceremonial functions in addition to purely economic ones, such a characteristic does not rule out its use as money considering the many ceremonial aspects of money today. Likely, shell beads in the South Pacific performed some, if not most, of the functions commonly ascribed to money.

Why did a money-like system of shell-bead exchange develop in the South Pacific? An answer to this question is found in Malinowski's initial impression of Trobriand islanders as sea-going Argonauts who traveled in canoes to trade across the open ocean. Many items that were traded between islands were specialized goods produced in certain parts of the archipelago (Macintyre, 1983a). Stone axe heads were produced from local stones on Muyuw island, for example, while pigs were considered a special export from Bwanabwana. Canoes from Gawa were also highly valued and traded throughout the region. *Spondylus* shell beads were themselves a specialized product that were procured and produced on Russell Island. Considering this interisland complementarity and the patchiness of resource distribution across the archipelago, trade currencies would have been carried by traders for exchanges across the entire region. Shell valuables perfectly fit this need, being durable, easily portable on a canoe (unlike, for example, pigs), and requiring considerable labor in order to produce. Shell beads would have provided transferability and divisibility for high-status goods such as canoes or pigs that would have been difficult to exchange otherwise. The money-like nature of shell valuables is also notable by the fact that they could be exchanged for modern currencies, although paper money was often of limited use on islands far from governmental centers (Macintyre, 1983a; Szabó, 2018). Shell valuables can thus be seen as an excellent portable currency in the long-distance, open-ocean trading networks of the South Pacific.

The use of shell valuables to conduct trade over long distances appears as a shared characteristic between Neolithic Europe and the South Pacific of the early twentieth century. In both cases, traders crossed considerable geographic, political, and cultural boundaries to acquire resources unavailable in their home areas. Beads made from *Spondylus* and other shells provided the medium to facilitate such exchange, being both portable and durable. It is highly likely that in Neolithic Europe, as in the twentieth-century Trobriands, the need to accrue prestige and display status also played a central role in the trade and exchange of shell valuables. Most transactions involving *kitomwa*, especially high-status valuables such as *soulava* and *mwali*, were in politically important exchanges involving blood debts, marriages, and funerals, or for the purchase of other prestigious items such as canoes or pigs. Considering that such political-economic transactions comprised the majority of nonsubsistence economic doings in Trobriand society, however, the importance and centrality of shell beads for the functioning of the region's economic system is difficult to question. Unfortunately, the antiquity of the European example and disagreements in the literature between Malinowski and subsequent anthropologists of the Trobriands make it difficult to determine exactly to what extent shell beads functioned like money in these cases. In the next section, I examine another example where shell beads were traded over vast geographic areas, and the scholarly consensus on their use of money is somewhat more clear-cut.

3 North America

All these Indians are fond of trafficking and commerce . . . In their trading they use beads for money. The beads are strung on long threads, arranged according to their value. The unit of exchange is a ponco of beads, which is two turns of the strings about the wrist and the extended third finger.

José Longinos Martínez in 1792, translated by Simpson (1961: 54–55), writing about the Chumash

The rich archaeological, ethnographic, and historical record of North America provides an abundance of information regarding the use of shell beads across the continent. Compared to the examples of shell beads discussed in Section 2, the historical record makes it clear that some forms of shell beads (especially wampum, see Section 3.2) were accepted as legal tender during colonial times in several European settlements (Peña, 2003; Shell, 2013). In addition, there is abundant archaeological information detailing a long history of shell-bead use, together with specialized production and cases of long-distance trade. Our task, therefore, is to determine to what degree monetary use of shell beads predated the colonial period and how extensive such use may have been. Drawing from the discussion in Section 1 on the role of money as a social technology, I argue in this section that Indigenous cultures across North America used shell beads to expand their economic capacities in both elite political-economic systems as well as more common daily transactions. As we shall see, shell money connected economies from distant parts of the continent, being produced on the coasts and then traded far and wide across North America's vast interior (Smith & Fauvelle, 2015). Shell money was a lubricating feature in long-distance trade systems of precolonial and early historic North America. It tied together distant places into a continent-spanning Indigenous known world stretching from coast to coast.

Almost everywhere that European colonialists went in North America, they encountered Indigenous peoples eager to conduct trade in shell beads (Figure 8). From purchases of land and provisions between Dutch settlers and Algonquian peoples in the Northeast to the many exchanges between Spanish Manila galleon crews and Californian peoples on the Pacific coast, examples abound of transactions between Indigenous peoples and Europeans denominated in beads. The Europeans involved in these exchanges saw beads as a local money, as evidenced by numerous texts detailing the exchange rates of various goods valued in quantities of beads. Beads were so ubiquitously accepted that Europeans soon began producing their own versions in glass, with Venetian craft guilds developing and specializing the mass production of beads by drawing out long glass tubes that were then cut and polished into beads by the tens of thousands and shipped on European vessels to all corners of the world (Blair, 2015). By the sixteenth and seventeenth centuries, demand for shell beads in the Americas was sufficient to move capital, build factories, and establish supply chains across early modern Europe. Shell beads were thus an

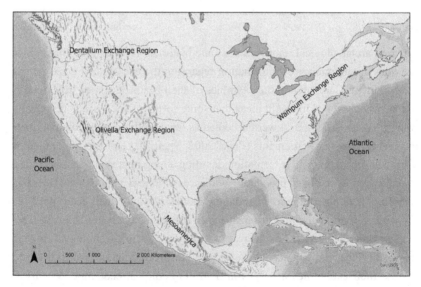

Figure 8 Shell-exchange regions in North America. Map by Mikael Fauvelle

initial component of the globalized economy that would rapidly dominate the early modern world.

Many cultures of North America produced and traded a wide array of shell-bead forms and types. In the Pacific Northwest, tusk-shaped *Dentalium* shells were collected from off the coasts of Vancouver Island and traded widely across the region, where they were often used as an exchange currency in interior regions (Clark, 1963; Sprague, 2004; Weld, 1963). In the Southeast, beads made from lightning whelk (*Busycon sinistrum*) and other gastropods from the Gulf of Mexico were widely traded to interior Mississippian polities, where they were traded in prestige networks and deposited in elite burials (Bissett & Claassen, 2016; Kozuch et al., 2017). On the Atlantic coast, whelk and clam shells were ground into beads called wampum, which were also widely traded through inland prestige networks and later incorporated into the economic systems of European colonialists (Bradley, 2011; Peña, 2003; Shell, 2013). Various shells were also broadly traded in Indigenous California, where they were used as an exchange currency in the northern and southern parts of the modern-day state (Burns, 2019; Gamble, 2020). Across the boundaries of these coastal areas and into the vast interior regions, shells were also widely traded, facilitating exchanges at great distances from their original point of manufacture (Kozuch, 2002; Smith & Fauvelle, 2015; Zappia, 2014). In the interests of space, this section focuses on two regions, southern California and the Northeast, where *Olivella* beads and wampum respectively represent two of the most discussed and debated forms of ancient North American shell money.

3.1 Money Beads from Pacific California

Shell money was central to Indigenous Californian economies. From the Early Holocene onward, shell beads were produced on southern California's islands and coasts and traded far and wide across the American West (Bennyhoff & Hughes, 1987; Fitzgerald et al., 2005). The scale of production increased steadily during the first millennium CE, and, by the end of the precolonial period, millions of beads were being produced by Chumash people on the Northern Channel Islands to be traded across the Santa Barbara Channel and beyond. The vast majority of these beads were made from the *Olivella* shells (technically *Callianax biplicata* but archaeologically known as *Olivella biplicata*), with only one cupped bead or possibly two disk beads being made from each individual shell (Gamble, 2020; King, 1990). The size and intensity of the southern California bead industry has intrigued archaeologists and anthropologists for decades and is a strong testament to the economic complexity of the Indigenous societies of the region.

Ethnohistorical sources describe the ways in which *Olivella* shell beads were used by Indigenous peoples in California (Bolton, 1930; King, 1976; Simpson, 1961). Perforated shell beads were usually strung by the hundreds into long strands, which were then wrapped around the head or neck and removed when they were needed for economic transactions (Figure 9). Value was determined by measuring lengths of bead strands, usually by wrapping the beads a set number of times around the width of one's hand or by measuring from one's elbow to one's fingertips (Kroeber, 1976). Some groups in California (for example, the Yurok) tattooed lines at set distances on their arms for the purposes

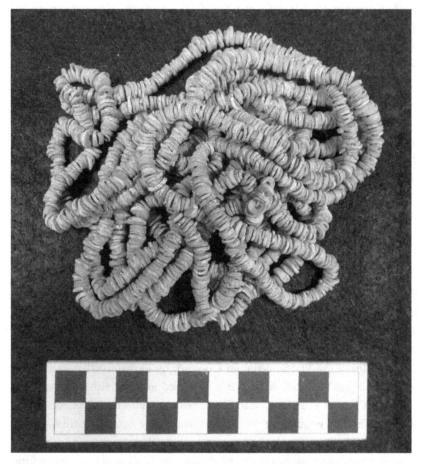

Figure 9 *Olivella* shell saucer beads from the Middle Period of the Santa Barbara Channel region. These were the first type of shell beads that were likely used as money in southern California, starting around 2,000 years ago (Gamble 2020). Image used courtesy of the Santa Barbara Museum of Natural History. Photo by Mikael Fauvelle

of measuring shell-bead strands, although this was not common among the Chumash (Kroeber, 1976). The practice of conducting trade in values set by lengths of bead strands was not limited to California but was also found in the Pacific Northwest (Clark, 1963), as well as across the American Southwest (Frisbie, 1974).

Many shell beads produced in southern California were made by the Chumash, who lived on the Northern Channel Islands and the adjacent mainland coast and interior ranges (see Figure 10). After around 1300 CE, Chumash society was organized into hierarchical, regional polities often described as chiefdoms in the archaeological literature (Arnold, 2001; Gamble, 2008; Kennett, 2005; King, 1990). The Chumash were hunter-fisher-foragers with abundant marine and terrestrial resources providing a rich resource base of intensive settlement on the region's islands, mainland, and in the interior (Fauvelle & Somerville, 2021a, 2021b). Villages were sedentary, with populations of up to 1,000 individuals (Gamble, 2008; Johnson, 1988). Economic activity and exchange between Chumash settlements was intense, with numerous goods exchanged between the islands, mainland coast, and interior mountain regions (Fauvelle & Perry, 2019, 2023; King, 1976). Oceangoing trade was conducted in advanced sewn-plank canoes (Arnold, 1995; Fauvelle, 2011;

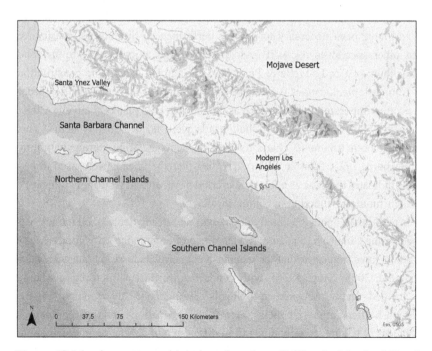

Figure 10 Islands, coasts, and interior of southern California. Map by Mikael Fauvelle

Gamble, 2002), and exchange was often mediated through the use of large amounts of shell-bead money.

Among the Chumash, strings of shell beads were exchanged for other goods in set units of value. In the epigraph that opens this section, for example, Longinos Martínez reports that a length of beads wrapped twice around the hand and extended to the end of one's third finger denoted a standard of value known as the ponco (Simpson, 1961: 54). Writing almost a half-century later, Anglo-American sailor Daniel Hill likewise reported that two-and-a-half hand-widths of beads was worth one Spanish real (one-eighth of a silver coin) (Woodward, 1934: 119). Highly standardized beads like those reported in these historical texts can be found in the archaeological record from at least 1,000 years ago (Gamble, 2020; see the following, and Figure 9), strongly suggesting a deep time depth for the practice of conducting exchange in values denominated through lengths of beads.

Ethnohistorical sources indicate that shell beads were used to conduct many economic activities in Chumash society, ranging from ceremonial exchanges between chiefs to daily trading for subsistence goods between commoners. All Chumash chiefs were members of the elite '*antap* society, into which they were invested as children by the payment of large amounts of shell-bead wealth by their parents (Blackburn, 1975; Gamble, 2020). One major obligation of Chumash chiefs was the organization of feasts, where shell-bead wealth would have been necessary to pay for performances by dancers, musicians, and other specialists, as well as to procure large amounts of surplus food (Blackburn, 1975; Fauvelle & Perry, 2023; Gamble, 2020). The construction of Chumash plank canoes would also have required shell-bead wealth in order to acquire important materials such as tar and redwood planks (Fauvelle, 2011; Hudson et al., 1978). Finally, shell beads were needed to pay debts. This included both tribute to chiefs as well as debts incurred during gambling (Blackburn, 1975; Gamble, 2020). The fact that shell beads were used to pay debts indicates their use as a form of deferred payment and is strongly indicative of their monetary function in Chumash society.

In addition to financing chiefly payments and settling debts, shell money was used by the Chumash to acquire a wide range of commoner daily goods. Many scholars have suggested that the Chumash economy had market characteristics (Gamble, 2008; King, 1976), with goods from different microregions being exchanged freely between individuals. Ethnohistorical accounts of the Chumash often emphasize their "mercantile" inclinations and detail numerous instances of Chumash individuals from different parts of the region meeting to conduct trade, often outside of the auspices of chiefly oversight or ceremonial activities (King, 1976). Chumash individuals from the interior would trade seeds, fruits, game, pelts, baskets, asphaltum, lithics, and many other goods to coastal and island people in exchange for items such stone bowls, fish, shellfish, and other marine goods (Fauvelle & Perry, 2019, 2023; King, 1976). All of these exchanges would be facilitated through the exchange of shell beads, which provided a critical lubricant for the economic interaction between adjacent microclimates. The use of shell money to conduct the exchange of daily and subsistence goods is another indication of its monetary functions among the Chumash.

Shell beads were produced by craft specialists who laboriously shaped and drilled beads from the walls of the small *Olivella* shell using chert microdrills (Figure 11) (Arnold, 1992; Arnold & Graesch, 2001). The time taken for a specialist to drill and shape a single bead varies from around fifteen minutes (Barbier, 2019) to an hour (Milliken et al., 2007: 110), exclusive of the time needed to procure the necessary tools and materials (Barbier, 2019; Gamble, 2020). Considering the hundreds of beads needed for every strand, these estimates make clear that shell-money production was a massive labor investment. Bead-making specialists were often sponsored by elites in a system that Arnold and Munns (1994) described as "attached specialization" due to the close association they see between increases in bead-making activity and the

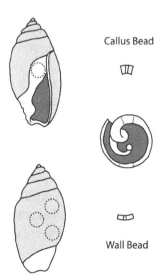

Figure 11 Diagram showing *Olivella* shell and location from which wall and callus beads were produced. Callus beads were made from the thickest portion of the shell, meaning only one bead per shell could be produced. Multiple thinner wall beads could be made from each shell, depending on the type of bead. Drawing by Mikael Fauvelle (see also Bennyhoff and Hughes, 1987: 89)

formation of Late Period chiefdoms. In the historic period, bead specialists could be of any gender, although it is unclear if this was the case in prehistoric times (Gamble, 2020: 6).

As emphasized in Section 1, monetary systems must have a means to control inflation in order to function as a dependable store of value. In the Chumash case, the high labor investment in grinding and drilling shell beads worked to keep values in check, as not everyone could afford to spend so much time producing beads. Large numbers of beads were also removed from circulation through burial and external trade. Most beads found by archaeologists in the Santa Barbara region come from burials where many thousands of beads are sometimes interred with single individuals (Gamble et al., 2001; King, 1990; Milliken et al., 2007). Counts of beads in burials increased during the Late Period, where most scholars see the strongest evidence for the monetary use of shell wealth (Gamble, 2020; King, 1990). Many thousands of beads were also removed from circulation through trade to exterior groups, with tens of thousands having been found in the interior valleys of California and beyond across the American West (Smith & Fauvelle, 2015). By removing beads from circulation through burial and external trade, values would be kept in check against the influx of new beads through production on the Channel Islands.

So many beads were produced on the Northern Channel Islands that they have often been referred to as the Santa Barbara regional "mint" (Arnold & Graesch, 2004: 7; Gamble, 2011: 232). Considering that *Olivella* shells are abundant on the mainland coast, the question of why shell-bead production came to be centered on the islands has been an enduring research topic in southern California archaeology (Arnold, 2012; Arnold & Graesch, 2001; Fauvelle, 2011, 2012, 2013, 2014). A once-popular argument that islanders produced shell beads in order to import subsistence resources from the mainland has faced considerable criticism (see Arnold & Martin, 2014; Fauvelle, 2013; Fauvelle et al., 2017; Gill et al., 2019). Recent arguments have focused on the needs of islanders to produce beads for ritual-exchange cycles or to acquire boat-building materials (Fauvelle, 2011; Fauvelle & Perry, 2019, 2023). Another possibility is that microdrills made from the high-quality chert found on the east end of Santa Cruz Island were preferred tools used by bead-making specialists (Nigra & Arnold, 2013). In any case, the centralization of bead production on the islands contributed to the centralization of power in the hands of canoe-owning chiefs who monopolized the exchange of commodities from the islands to the mainland.

Were *Olivella* shell beads used as money by the Chumash? Most scholars working in the region certainly seem to think so. For the past several decades, a broad consensus among archaeologists working in southern California has held that cupped *Olivella* "money beads" were used as currency by the Chumash during the Late and Historic periods (Arnold, 1995, 2001; Arnold & Graesch, 2001; Gamble, 2008, 2011, 2020; King, 1976, 1990). In a recent article, Gamble (2020) has compellingly argued that shell beads were money based on their standardization in size, the labor involved in their production, their distribution across the Chumash economy, and ethnohistorical accounts of their use in settling debts and conducting daily exchange. Considering the characteristics of money outlined in Section 1, I agree with Gamble (and many other scholars of ancient California) that the Chumash used shell beads as money. *Olivella* beads were highly transferable, storable, standardized, and avoided inflation through deposition in burials and trade to distant regions. Critically, they also greatly expanded the capacity of the Chumash economic system to get things done – by providing a means to facilitate trade over wide and disparate areas, to accrue wealth, and to finance the construction of highly advanced plank canoes.

When did the Chumash start using shell beads as money? Cupped beads made from the thick callus portion of the *Olivella* shell were the most labor-intensive type of bead to drill and are often referred to as "money beads" in the California archaeology literature (Arnold & Rachal, 2002; Brown et al., 2022; Gamble, 2020; King, 1976, 1990). These beads started to be used during the Transitional Period (ca. 1150 CE) and are found widely dispersed in archaeological contexts and burial areas, suggesting that most members of society had access to them (King, 1976, 1990). Recently, Gamble (2020) has pushed back the date of likely monetary use of shell beads in southern California by around 1,000 years, arguing that earlier saucer beads were likely used as money during the Middle Period. While saucer beads were not as labor-intensive to produce as cupped beads, they were also highly standardized. As shown by Gamble (2020: 101237), earlier saucer beads actually have a slightly smaller range of variation in size than do later cupped beads. Saucer beads were also traded far and wide, with tens of thousands found in Central California and the San Francisco Bay area (Burns, 2019; Gamble, 2020; Milliken et al., 2007), hundreds of kilometers distant from the Santa Barbara Channel. If one of the functions of Chumash money was to facilitate interregional trade, then saucer beads were likely filling this role by around 2,000 years ago.

The question of where Chumash shell beads were traded to is important for understanding their roles in regional political and economic histories. In order to combat inflation, shell money needs to be removed from circulation at a rate approximately matching that at which it is produced. Many of the shell beads produced on the Channel Islands were deposited in burials throughout the Chumash area. Many others, however, were removed from local circulation through trade to adjacent regions and beyond. This created an "export-oriented" economy, with demand for shell beads in exterior regions fueling increases in production in the Santa Barbara Channel (Fauvelle, 2011, 2014). As was previously mentioned, tens of thousands have been found in Central California and were likely transported there through trade networks dominated by the Yokuts of the San Joaquin Valley. Tens of thousands more were also carried east, where they circulated in a vast region across the American Southwest (Smith & Fauvelle, 2015; Zappia, 2014). Although the strongest evidence for the money-like use of shell beads in western North America comes from the Chumash region itself, ethnohistorical sources also suggest that Chumash beads were used as currency across this wide region in which they were traded.

Shell beads from the Pacific were the currency that fueled a vast trading and interaction region described as the "Interior World" of the American West (see Figure 12) (Zappia, 2014). Mojave traders were key middlemen in this network, carrying ceramics and textiles from the Puebloan Southwest to the California coast to trade in exchange for Chumash shell beads (Smith & Fauvelle, 2015). Several Spanish documents chronicle meeting Mojave trading parties either on or traveling to the California coast (Bolton, 1908, 1930; Earle, 2005), and the intensity of this trade was sufficient that it prompted Spanish attempts to control

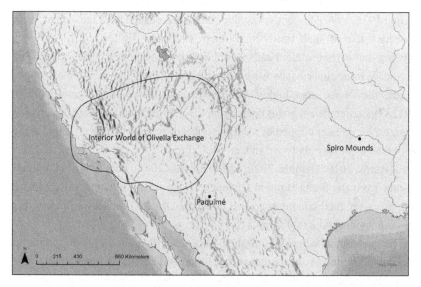

Figure 12 Map showing "Interior World" of *Olivella* shell-exchange region and other sites with large assemblages of shell beads discussed in Element. Map by Mikael Fauvelle

and regulate it (Earle, 2005). The archaeological signature of this exchange is represented by over 26,000 shell artifacts found in excavations in the interior Southwest, a number which likely represents only a small fraction of the true total, considering that many early excavations in the region did not record shell finds (Smith, 2002). Even further east, shells from the Pacific Ocean have been found at Mississippian sites in Alabama and Oklahoma, including some 13,948 *Olivella dama* shells at the Spiro Mounds site near the Mississippi river (Kozuch, 2002). Such finds indicate that the trade network for California shell reached over some 2,000 kilometers, spanning two-thirds of the North American continent.

What was all this California shell doing in the American Southwest and beyond? Many ethnohistorical accounts suggest that it was used as money. Adolph Bandelier (1890: 149), for example, wrote that Puebloan people used strings of shell beads as a "conventional currency", while Johan Bourke (1884: 254) described "perforated sea-shell beads" as being used as a form of commodity currency. The Zuni word for shell-bead strings was *hishi*, and they were also used as currency in their territory during the nineteenth century (Frisbie, 1974). In some cases, set exchange rates were recorded by travelers and early ethnographers. Earnest Beaglehole (1937: 84), for example, wrote that one string of shell beads could purchase two cotton blankets among the Hopi, while Grenville Goodwin wrote that one shell-bead string could be exchanged for a buckskin among the Zuni and Apache (Goodwin, 1942: 81). Although it is difficult to project these ethnographic cases backward in time, if we consider that the trade of California shell into the Southwest greatly intensified between 1150 CE and 1300 CE, it is possible that money-like use of shell beads in the region may date to this period. This corresponds to the Transitional Period in California and the Hohokam Classic Period in the Southwest, times during which both areas were undergoing transformations toward greater social complexity (Smith & Fauvelle, 2015).

The importance of shell beads in facilitating exchange between and within cultural groups across the American West is evocative of the concept that money could develop from a medium of exchange. Standardized saucer and cupped shell beads produced by Chumash bead specialists would have been highly fungible, working as a uniform valuable well suited for exchange across cultural boundaries (e.g. Earle, 2018). In the desert regions of the Southwest, shells would also have been naturally scarce, ensuring their worth as a store of value. The existence of long-distance trade and travel in the region is also well documented, with known cases of individual trading parties traveling north and south between the Mexican border and Kansas and east and west between the California coast and New Mexico (Kehoe, 2002; Smith & Fauvelle, 2015).

Shell money would have been a key piece of social technology facilitating this widespread interior world of intensive interaction, allowing travelers to conduct exchanges in familiar currency over an area spanning thousands of kilometers. In the next section, I discuss a case where shell beads were traded over even more vast distances in Eurasia and Africa, but first I briefly consider another famous case of shell-bead use in North America – wampum used across the American Northeast.

3.2 Wampum from the Atlantic Northeast

Wampum is a shortened form of the term *wampumpeag*, which was an anglicized version of the Indigenous Massachusetts term for a string of white shell beads. Wampum consisted of tubular beads carved from quahog (*Busycotypus canaliculatus*) and whelk (*Mercenaria mercenaria*) shells that were strung and woven into patterned belts (Figure 13). Most wampum was white, but beads could also be purple or black, depending on the shell used. In contemporary North America, wampum is one of the best-known forms of Indigenous shell beads, largely due to its role in the early economy of the British colonies that formed the United States. Given their ease of use for exchange with Indigenous people and the general lack of European coinage in circulation, American colonists adopted wampum as currency, with the beads becoming legal tender in New England and North Carolina in the seventeenth and early eighteenth centuries (Peña, 2003; Shell, 2013). Before adoption by Europeans, wampum circulated widely across the Indigenous Northeast and was a critical component of the political economy of Iroquoian Confederacies, including the Haudenosaunee and the Wendat (Bradley, 2011). Much like *Olivella* shells from the Pacific, wampum in the Northeast tied together a geographic area with similar forms of exchange and concepts of material value.

The production and exchange of shell objects have a long history on the east coast of North America. Shell beads are found in the Northeast from the beginning of the Late Archaic period some 4,500 years ago (Ceci, 1982; Fenton, 1998). Between the Middle and Late Woodlands periods (ca. 200 BCE to 1000 CE), shell beads are increasingly common at sites across the region (Ceci, 1982). Hundreds of shell beads are found in Hopewell period burials, while later Mississippian sites contain both Atlantic and Pacific shell beads by the thousands (Kozuch, 2002; Kozuch et al., 2017). As in the California case study, most shell beads were polished and drilled by specialists on the coast and then traded to inland groups. In later precolonial periods, shell-bead production was centered on Chesapeake Bay, and trade in beads flowed inland following rivers such as the Potomac, Hudson, Delaware, and

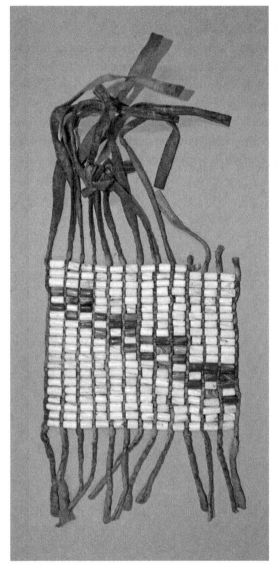

Figure 13 Wampum belt. Date unknown. © The Trustees of the British Museum

Susquehanna (Bradley, 2011; Ceci, 1982). Early wampum beads were univer-
sally white, with the first purple wampum being produced in the early seventeenth century (Bradley, 2011; Ceci, 1982). In later periods, individual beads
were valued at different rates, with purple and black beads being worth two to
three times as much as white ones (Jacobs, 1949). Despite a long history of the
use and exchange of shell goods, wampum production increased considerably

around the mid-sixteenth century, likely corresponding with early European contact (Bradley, 2011; Fenton, 1998).

Wampum circulated widely within the Haudenosaunee Iroquois Confederacy that dominated the political landscape across much of the Northeast between the mid-fifteenth and the end of the eighteenth century (Figure 14) (Fenton, 1998). Like other contemporary Iroquoian-speaking confederacies such as the Wendat, the Haudenosaunee was characterized by a corporate political organization dominated by coalition building and consensus politics (Birch & Hart, 2018; Trigger, 1987). Each village was comprised of one or more clans, which were in

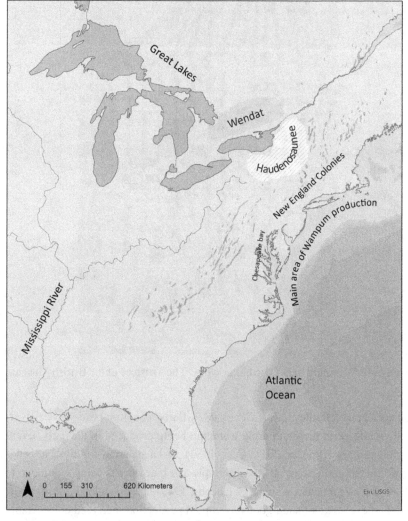

Figure 14 Map of regions discussion in Section 3.2. Map by Mikael Fauvelle

turn represented by two elected leaders – one who led in matters of war and the other who acted as a civil leader. These leaders were usually men but could occasionally be women (Birch & Hart, 2018: 19). Women were also present at elections in council and clan meetings. Leadership positions were not inherited but were instead elected by other prominent individuals based on the qualities of individual leaders (Trigger, 1987). Tribal nations that comprised Iroquoian confederacies held councils made up of clan leaders, who were also elected in the same fashion. It was these individuals who were often in charge of negotiating treaties with other Indigenous or European groups (Trigger, 1987). Decisions on every political level – from clan to village to nation – were driven by consensus rather than majority vote, making the skills of persuasion, gift giving, and alliance building critical elements of political life (Birch & Hart, 2018; Trigger, 1987).

Wampum had many roles central to the functioning of the Iroquois political-economic system (Bradley, 2011). Strings of shell beads were used to call clan leaders to meetings or councils and also served as a physical reminder of the political constitution of the Iroquois league, which according to legend involved the weaving of a wampum belt (Bradley, 2011; Fenton, 1998). Wampum was central to the functioning of ritual exchange and diplomacy and was almost always exchanged during meetings between leaders or at civic ceremonies and public events (Bradley, 2011). Gifts were also commonly given in the form of wampum, as the shells were seen as representing light, health, and success (Bradley, 2011; Hamell, 1986). Taken together, these functions were critical to the consensus and coalition building that was central to Iroquois political life. Without the flow of wampum to seal deals, curry favor, and form alliances, the corporate political system of the Iroquois Confederacy is unlikely to have worked. The social technology represented by shell-bead money was therefore central to the functioning of the complex Iroquois political world.

One function that wampum did not fulfill in Iroquois societies – at least until their close integration into European market economics – was as a currency for daily exchange. This has led scholars such as David Graeber (1996, 2011, 2012) to argue that Indigenous wampum should not be considered as true money. Instead, Graeber (2012) argues that wampum was a "social currency" that functioned primarily to transform social relationships rather than to exchange or accumulate material goods. In many ways, Graeber is right – the primary function of wampum was indeed to create and maintain social relationships between people. As was discussed in Section 1, however, contemporary money is not purely transactional but also mediates numerous social relationships. The fact that few daily goods were purchased with wampum should also not be surprising, considering the subsistence economy of Indigenous life in the precolonial Northeast. Farming, hunting, and crafting were largely carried out on the village or clan level with little need to procure many material goods from outside groups in a market system (Trigger, 1987). This parallels the role of money in many early Eurasian societies, where serfs and commoners met many of their own subsistence and craft needs without the use of metal coinage. If we see money as a continuum, the centrality of wampum to the political economy of the Iroquois system can be seen as paralleling that of many early European states where most money flowed within the boundaries of elite political networks.

The relative lack of daily or mercantile transactions conducted in wampum in the Northeast stands in clear contrast to the California case study. As was discussed in Section 3.1, a primary role of Chumash money beads was to facilitate market-like exchanges for food and craft goods. Numerous ethnohistorical descriptions show that individuals would travel from different regions of the Chumash world to major villages where they could conduct trades demarcated in quantities of shell beads. This was also the case for the interior regions of the American West, where Pacific shells flowed directly along major trade routes and were used to facilitate exchange between different ethnic and political groups. Of course, Chumash money beads also had political implications, as they were used to pay debts and provide for chiefly functions such as holding feasts and building canoes. In this sense, *Olivella* shells from the Pacific were likely further along the money continuum than wampum in the Northeast. For the Northeast case study, wampum only reached its most money-like form when exchanged across the strong cultural boundary separating Indigenous Americans from European colonizers.

One area where wampum and *Olivella* money beads were similar was in the way in which their value was maintained against inflation. In both cases, the high labor cost of producing beads together with natural scarcity in interior regions worked to maintain the value of shell money. Iroquoian groups in the Northeast interior and Puebloan groups in the American Southwest had to acquire coastal shells through trade, giving them an intrinsic value through scarcity. The standardized production, small size, and durable nature of shells also worked to make the beads both fungible and easily transportable, making them well suited to fulfill several of the functions of money. Value was also maintained in both cases through the deposition of shell beads in burials. In the American West, this system was able to maintain the value of shell beads well after European contact, with Yokuts and Chumash people conducting exchanges in shell beads up until the early twentieth century (Latta, 1949). This was not the case for wampum, which was subjected to runaway inflation and the collapse of the currency's value following the intensification of production by coastal European groups toward the end of the eighteenth century (Bradley, 2011).

Another major difference between the two case studies described in this section concerns differences in scales of political organization. Precolonial Chumash societies are commonly described as chiefdoms (Arnold, 2001; Gamble, 2008), while various forms of corporate- and network-oriented Southwest polities were also fairly local in the scale of their regional integration (Feinman et al., 2000). The Iroquois Confederacy, on the other hand, was a vast and highly complex regional political organization that for several centuries was able to compete on a peer level with early European colonial states. It is noteworthy that in comparing these two examples, the smaller-scale polities of the American West were the ones where the use of shell beads was the most money-like in character. On the east coast, on the other hand, colonial inter-locutors from European states quickly adopted and transformed Indigenous shell currency, using it to facilitate the economies of their colonial governments. The differences between these two examples show that, while the use of money-like currency is clearly not exclusive to state societies, it certainly can facilitate the expansion of state actors and groups. In the next section, we examine a case where shell beads were traded over an even larger geographical space and were directly involved with the economic formations of archaic states and empires.

4 Cowrie Money in Asia and Africa

The commoner Ju Bai received from Qiu Wei a jade tablet which was worth 80 peng [double strings of cowrie shells] in exchange for ten tian [parcels of land] from his estate, Ju also received two pieces of red coral, a pair of kid knee-caps, and a parade belt, all worth 20 peng, in exchange for three tian from his estate.
Inscription on Qiu Wei Bronze from Dongjia, Qishan County, China. Zhou Dynasty, 915 BCE. Translation from Thierry (2018: 337)

While the Kula ring may be one of the most-discussed examples of shell exchange in anthropology, and wampum is famous for its role in the history of early colonial America, no form of shell money has been as widely used throughout history as the money cowrie (Figure 15). Even the cowrie's scientific name, *Monetaria moneta*, points to its acknowledged use as a form of money. Numerous historical accounts show that cowrie shells functioned as money across areas of Africa and Asia into early modern times, while archaeological records show intensive production and widespread exchange of the money cowrie across Asia by at least 1000 BCE. The question, then, is where and when did cowrie shells begin to take on the various attributes of money and transition from a valuable and prestigious trade good to a money-like medium of exchange.

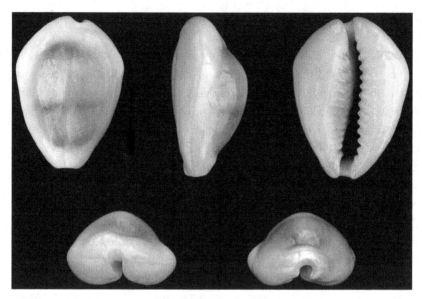

Figure 15 *Monetaria moneta*. Photo by H. Zell. From Wikimedia Commons. Used under Creative Commons Attribution-Share Alike 3.0 Generic License

Collected by the millions in the Maldives and traded from the Indian Ocean to all corners of Eurasia and Africa, the money cowrie represents a global history of trade and interaction. It comes from a small sea snail found in the tropical waters of the Indian and Pacific Oceans (Figure 16). When alive, the cowrie subsists mainly on algae in shallow waters and reefs. The cowrie shell is around 3 cm long and can be nearly completely enveloped by the foot and mantle of the living cowrie. By itself, the shell is shiny and hard with a characteristic long and narrow opening lined with pronounced denticules. The shell is naturally quite durable, lightweight, and easy to transport. Even Karl Polanyi has noted the cowrie's suitability for currency, writing that "cowrie shells can be poured, sacked, shoveled, hoarded in heaps, kept buried in the solid, chuted like gravel – [yet] they remain clean, dainty, stainless, polished, and milk-white" (Polanyi, 1969: 178). These physical attributes allow cowries to circulate for decades or even centuries without discernible change in form or value.

The cowrie shares many characteristics with other shells discussed in this Element that make it well suited for use as a form of money. In addition to its durability and ease of transport, its unique shape and source area make it hard to counterfeit or substitute. Unlike many other forms of shell money, the cowrie was often used in an unmodified form. Rather than deriving value from the labor invested in the manufacture of beads, the worth of cowrie shells was largely derived from their scarcity in the predominantly inland regions in which they

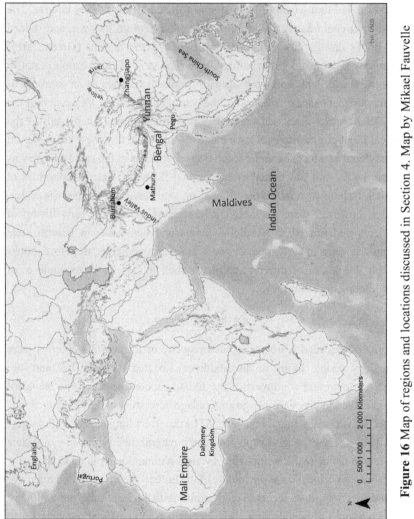

Figure 16 Map of regions and locations discussed in Section 4. Map by Mikael Fauvelle

were used. Although Africa, India, and China have long coasts, they are distant from the main areas of cowrie production and have vast inland areas with no access to the sea. In this sense, the cowrie shares an important characteristic with the shell money of North America that was produced on coasts and highly valued in the continent's vast interior.

The widespread use of cowrie shells by many cultures and across many periods has led to a wealth of scholarship focused on the money cowrie. The cowrie shell could easily be the focus of an Element on its own, and indeed many books discuss cowrie money in different world regions (Green, 2019; Hogendorn & Johnson, 1986; Yang, 2018). The goal of this section is not to repeat these excellent works but instead to present cowries as an example of shell money that exists on one end of the continuum (Section 1). Several of the examples of shells discussed previously performed some, but not all, of the classical functions of money. I have made the argument that these cases should be considered as a form of social technology that exists in the same category as modern money and functioned to expand and facilitate ancient economies in a similar fashion to how euros, dollars, or yen move our economies today. Cowries, however, were unambiguously seen as money in many historical documents and moved in parallel to coins and banknotes in several state economic systems in early modern times. Discussing cowries, therefore, bookends our discussion of different forms of shell money as an example most clearly like modern currency.

4.1 Maldives

For most of recorded history, the vast majority of the world's cowries were supplied by people living in the Maldives. Located between 750 and 400 kilometers south and southwest of the Indian subcontinent and the island of Sri Lanka, the Maldives are a large archipelago consisting of 1,192 coral islands grouped into 26 atolls found in an area 871 kilometers long and 130 kilometers wide. This vast marine landscape provided a natural defense, as few outsiders were able to navigate the archipelago's waters without local pilots. Conversely, the island chain's location in the middle of the Indian Ocean facilitated intensive and sustained long-distance trade connections with Africa, India, and Southeast Asia. Thousands of islands with vast reaches of warm and shallow waters also provided the perfect habitat for the money cowrie.

Some scholars argue that the origin of the name "Maldives" comes from Sanskrit and means necklace islands, pointing to the archipelago's importance as a source of shell beads (Yang, 2018: 20). Cowrie shells are abundant here and can easily be collected from shallow waters and reefs. Many historic accounts describe leaving palm branches in the water and then collecting cowries that have attached themselves to the leaves (Yang, 2018). Shells were then laid out on the beach in the sun or dug into the sand where the flesh of the cowrie would decompose, leaving only the white shell to be washed in the sea and amassed. This allowed vast numbers of cowries to be collected without the need to dive into the sea or to invest much labor processing. The hundreds of islands of the Maldives also provided abundant cowrie habitats that could easily accommodate the intensification of collection. As shells were counted as individual units, smaller shells were more highly prized, as higher numbers could be transported in the same ship's cargo space (Hogendorn & Johnson, 1986). This is one of the reasons why the smaller *Monetaria moneta* available in the Maldives was preferred over several larger cowrie species.

Untold millions of cowrie beads were exported from the Maldives throughout the past two millennia, reaching markets across Asia and Africa. Visiting the Maldives in 1619, for example, French navigator François Pyrard de Laval recorded seeing "30 or 40 whole ships loaded with them [cowries] without other cargo" (Litster, 2016: 9). According to de Laval, all the ships and the millions of shells in their holds were destined for Bengal in the Mughal Empire. Several centuries earlier, the traveler Ibn Battuta also recorded massive exchanges of cowrie money, writing that cowries were "used for buying and selling at the rate of four hundred thousand shells for a gold dinar" and that they were sold "in exchange for rice to the people of Bengal" (Yang, 2018: 27). Ibn Battuta also noted that cowries were traded and used as currency in Africa. Chinese and Portuguese traders visited the Maldives to acquire cowrie shells, and European ships increasingly carried them to Africa, where they were more and more central in financing the slave trade during the early modern period (Hogendorn & Johnson, 1986).

Why did the Maldives become a center for cowrie production when they also occur naturally throughout the Indian Ocean and parts of the Pacific? Part of the answer is the sheer abundance of cowries that can be found on the islands. With over 1,000 coral atolls and nearly endless shallow waters and reefs, it was relatively easy to procure vast quantities of cowries there. The warm waters of the Maldives also meant that the cowries grew smaller shells, increasing their value (Yang, 2018). Another critical factor was the broader economy of the Maldives. Although the region also exported dried fish and coconut-fiber rope, the small islands were lacking in many finished products and materials, necessitating the importation of a wide range of goods. As cowries were cheap and plentiful on the islands and in high demand elsewhere, intensifying the production of shell money provided an easy way for the Maldives to alleviate its demand for imported goods. The island chain's location in the middle of the

Indian Ocean also facilitated the transport of cowries to many different locations in Africa and Asia.

That islands became the center for the production of shell money is a characteristic shared between the Maldives and the Chumash case study discussed in Section 3. While both the Maldives and the Channel Islands were rich in marine resources and could support relatively large populations, their small sizes coupled with patchy resource distribution meant that they needed to import several key resources. In the Chumash case, these included canoe building materials and ritual goods, while in the Maldives islanders lacked metals, ceramics, and other finished products. Specializing in the production of shell money provided both island chains with an economic niche that allowed them to acquire needed goods from continental resource areas. This comparison can also be extended to the Kula valuables discussed in Section 2, where resource differences between islands encouraged long-distance interisland trade. Islands often represent bounded cultural and political regions, such that the development of shell money helped facilitate trade between islands and adjacent coasts with different resources and ambitions. Island-based shell money may be a common and shared crosscultural phenomenon.

When did cowrie money start to be produced and exported from the Maldives? Unfortunately, the answer remains unclear, largely due to poor archaeological coverage of the earliest periods of the island's occupation (Litster, 2016). Ocean modeling suggests that early Austronesian pioneers traveling from Indonesia to Madagascar may have passed through the Maldives, but any archaeological evidence for such layovers is currently lacking (Fitzpatrick & Callaghan, 2008; Litster, 2016). The earliest secure dates for habitation in the Maldives come from the fourth century CE, associated with an island colonization from either Sri Lanka or southern India (Litster, 2016). By this time, cowries were already being used as currency in parts of India (Yang, 2018), suggesting that exploitation of the region's abundance in cowries might have been one of the motivations behind the initial occupation (Mikkelsen, 2000). Experimentation with cowrie money began in China up to a millennium earlier, however, suggesting that, while the Maldives dominated later shell production, the world's first money cowries probably came from elsewhere.

4.2 China

Cowrie shells have held a special place in Chinese political economies ever since the Neolithic. Hoards of cowries have been found in excavated sites. Inscriptions on bronzes describing economic exchanges denominated in cowries indicate the importance of the cowrie shell in early Chinese economies dating before 1045 BCE. Most scholars agree that by the Zhou Dynasty, cowrie shells were being used as money in ancient China (Andersson, 1932; Peng & Zhu, 1995; Thierry, 2018; cf. Yang, 2018; Yao, 2010; Yung-Ti, 2003). The importance of the cowrie was such that during the second millennium BCE, bronze imitation cowries were used as one of China's first metal currencies. Even today, the Chinese character for shells, 貝 (*bèi*), is synonymous with money (Figure 17). This linguistic connection between money and cowries is shared in other Asian languages including Thai and Khmer. These widespread

Oracle script
(~1250-1000 BC)

Bronze script
Late Shang dynasty
(~1100 BC)

Bronze script
Early Western Zhou
(~1000 BC)

Bronze script
Mid Western Zhou
(~900 BC)

Seal script
Chu (Warring States:
475-221 BC)

Seal script
Shuowen
(~100 AD)

Clerical script
Eastern Han
Dynasty
(25-220 AD)

Traditional script
Modern

Simplified script
Modern

Figure 17 Evolution of Chinese character for money, *bèi*. Note the similarity to the cowrie shell. Chinese characters from Chinese Character Wiki. Used under Creative Commons Attribution-Share Alike 4.0 International License

connections between cowries and money indicate a long history of importance for the cowrie shell across East and Southeast Asia.

Cowries were imported into China by the end of the third millennium BCE (Li, 2018; Peng & Zhu, 1995), and early use of cowries was concentrated in northern China along the Upper and Middle regions of the Yellow River, far from the sources of cowrie shells. The earliest cowrie finds are associated with the Neolithic Majiayao culture from the Upper Yellow River and date to between 3300 and 2000 BCE. They are also common in sites from the Late Neolithic Longshang Culture, especially in the Middle Yellow River basin region. Longshang period cowries are often found with perforations indicating that they were used as jewelry or adornment (Li, 2018). They are common in burials, suggesting an association with mortuary rituals. Li (2018: 107) has suggested that cowries during the Longshang period represented wealth and esoteric knowledge and may have been worn together with beads from other precious materials such as carnelian and turquoise as a part of shamanic traditions that originated in North and Central Asia.

Early Chinese cowries were likely traded over a great distance from the Indian Ocean. Sea temperatures off the coast of China (including the South China Sea) would have been too low during this period to support the growth of cowries, suggesting an origin elsewhere (Peng & Zhu, 1995). Support for trade from the Indian Ocean can be found in the distribution of archaeological cowrie shells, with more found at inland and highland sites than along the coast, suggesting trade from the west likely originating in India or through or via Central Asian trade networks (Li, 2018). Although the Maldives are unlikely to have been inhabited during the earliest periods of cowrie use in China, the shells could have come from other islands or from the coast of the Indian subcontinent. Yang (2018: 128) suggests that, by the end of the first millennium BCE, these shells followed a "Cowrie Road" which predated the Silk Road and connected India, China, and Central Asia as part of a large Bronze Age interaction sphere.

The use of cowries increased drastically during the second and first millennium BCE (Peng & Zhu, 1995; Thierry, 2018). During the Shang and Zhou dynasties, cowries were commonly deposited in burials, sometimes in very large quantities. One spectacular example is the burial of Fu Hao, the twelfth-century BCE wife of the Shang Dynasty king Wuding, who was found with 6,800 cowries (Yang, 2018). At the Western Zhou site of Zhangjiapo near Xi'an, 81 percent of all burials across the site contained cowries (Yang, 2018). During the Western and Eastern Zhou periods, the use of cowries in northern China was also at its most widespread, with finds across the Yellow River basin and in territories adjacent to those controlled by the Zhou Dynasty (Thierry, 2018). The use of cowries decreased in the second half of the first millennium BCE, as shells were replaced by metal coinage. In the southern region of Yunnan, however, cowrie importation continued, with hundreds of thousands found in burials dating to the second-century BCE Dian culture (Yang, 2018).

Were cowries used as money in ancient China? Texts inscribed on Shang and Zhou Dynasty divination bones and bronze vessels can help us answer this question. As described by Thierry (2018), early texts generally describe cowries as rewards for services to a king or lord, but later texts on bronze vessels during the Zhou Dynasty encompass a wide range of economic and social transactions. These exchanges include the purchase of land, the payment for services, and the exchange of goods (Thierry, 2018: 338). As is seen in the opening epigraph for this section, these transactions took place in units of *peng* (朋) which were corded double strands of cowrie shells. Excavated examples of *peng* contain two strands of five shells each, suggesting that one *peng* denoted ten cowries (Thierry, 2018; Yang, 2018). The first recorded use of the character *mai* (买), meaning to buy or purchase, also dates to the Western Zhou period and records the sale of a jade object for fifty *peng* on the Kang ding bronze (Yang, 2018: 138; Yung-Ti, 2003: 9). The fact that many different descriptions denote values for various items in terms of *peng* suggests that cowries were being used as a unit of account and a medium of exchange during Zhou period China and is a strong case for their use as money. It is notable that early Chinese historians also agreed, including first-century BCE Han writers such as Sima Qian and Huan Kuan, who both named cowrie shells as forms of early currency (Yang, 2018: 137).

Most modern scholars agree that cowrie shells were one of the first forms of money in early China (Andersson, 1932; Peng & Zhu, 1995; Thierry, 2018; Von Glahn, 1996; Yao, 2010). Several scholars, however, have recently argued against this consensus (Yang, 2018; Yung-Ti, 2003). Analyzing Zhou bronze texts, Yung-Ti (2003) argues that most inscriptions describe gifts given and received between royalty and members of the elite, rather than daily exchanges or regular purchases. He argues that this suggests that cowries may have been a unit of account but not a medium of exchange (Yung-Ti, 2003: 7). Yang (2018) agrees with this assessment and adds that the great distance over which cowries would have been imported from the Indian Ocean may have made them impractical for use as a regular currency. Although both scholars agree that cowries were an important part of Chinese monetary history, they argue that "true" money did not originate until the advent of widely circulating metal currencies during the second half of the first millennium BCE.

I agree, however, with the consensus that cowries were used as money in ancient China during the Shang and Zhou Dynasties. Throughout this Element, I have argued that money should be seen as a continuum, fulfilling different functions as needed for the economic systems in which they were invented and used. In ancient China, the fact that cowries were denominated at set standards of value and facilitated a wide range of economic transactions strongly suggests that they were used as money.

The argument that cowries could not have been "true" money as they circulated largely among the elite is evocative of the arguments made by Graeber (1996, 2001, 2011, 2012) as discussed in Sections 1 and 3. As was argued there, the political economy of ancient societies was largely dominated by elite activities, suggesting that most monetary exchanges would take place in precisely those settings. In the case of ancient China, this is further complicated by the fact that almost all texts regarding cowrie exchanges come from elite contexts, obscuring our ability to understand how cowries were used in nonelite society. The argument that cowries could not have been used as money since the distance involved in their procurement from India was too great seems unconvincing, as it was precisely long-distance exchange that maintained the value of shell monies in other world regions such as the interior of North America (Section 3). Given the dual role of cowries in ancient China as a unit of value and a medium of exchange, it seems highly likely that cowries were used as money in ancient China by at least the Zhou Dynasty and possibly even earlier.

Cowrie use in ancient China is connected to many counterfeit and imitation shells that have been found in archaeological sites (Figure 18). Imitation cowries were made from steatite, clay, clam shell, bone, lead, and bronze (Thierry, 2018: 339). Imitation cowries first appear during Neolithic times but greatly increase in frequency during the Western Zhou period. By the middle of the first millennium BCE, many tombs contained more imitation cowries than real ones (Yang, 2018: 131). The fact that counterfeit cowries greatly increased

Figure 18 Stone imitation cowrie. Date unknown. © The Trustees of the British Museum

in circulation in the centuries following good textual documentation for use of cowries as a unit of value could be seen as another line of evidence suggesting their adoption as money during this period. If this were the case, however, it suggests that the value of cowries was dependent on their scarcity and that little control by the Zhou state existed over shell money. Following Gresham's law, "bad money drives out the good," the increasing circulation of imitation cowries would have had a strong impact on the stability of their value. This likely played an important factor in their gradual replacement by metal money (including bronze cowries and coins stamped with the *bèi* and *peng* characters) in northern China toward the end of the Eastern Zhao period.

In the southern region of Yunnan, cowries were used as money for millennia, circulating up to the middle of the seventeenth century CE (Yang, 2018). Numerous historical texts detail the use of cowries in Yunnan for market exchanges in the Dali Kingdom (937–1253 CE) as well as during the subsequent Yuan and Ming periods. Marco Polo, for example, visited Yunnan in the thirteenth century and described the use of cowrie money in detail, including the fact that cowries originated in India (and originally the Maldives). Imperial attempts during both the Yuan and Ming dynasties to replace cowries with paper or metal money failed, seemingly due to the deep popularity of cowries for daily exchanges (Yang, 2018: 107, 114). Inflation was a major problem for cowrie money in Yunnan, however, as the difference in value between cowries in the Yangtze Delta (where they were not used as currency) and inland Yunnan was enormous. Starting as early as 1276, officials in Yunnan realized the problems of runaway inflation and began a series of proclamations prohibiting the use of cowries imported from the east in favor of local cowries that had arrived from the west through trade with India (Yang, 2018: 205–206). By the mid-seventeenth century, inflationary pressures proved to be too great, resulting in the collapse of the currency. The persistence of cowrie use as a currency in Yunnan is strongly tied to the region's role as China's gateway for trade with India and Southeast Asia, where cowries continued to be used until modern times.

4.3 India and Southeast Asia

The word cowrie comes to the English language from the Hindi or Urdu word *kaur*, which is derived from the Sanskrit word *kaparda* (Yang, 2018). The importance of cowries in ancient India can be noted from the fact that two Vedic gods, Pushan and Rudra-Siva (predecessor to Shiva), are described in the *Rigveda* as having hair braided like cowrie shells (Srinivasan, 1983: 544). Such textual references suggest that cowries were of religious significance in ancient

India as early as the second millennium BCE (cf. Parpola, 2020). In later periods, cowrie shells would come to take on economic importance, used for money on the Indian subcontinent from at least the middle of the first millennium CE through the early decades of the twentieth century (Yang, 2018). For much of this history, Bengal was the center for cowrie use and trade, receiving shells by the millions from the Maldives and shipping them via land and sea to far reaches of the African and Eurasian world.

Archaeological finds of cowrie shells are rare at early sites in India, although some have been reported at Bronze Age Harappan sites in the Indus Valley (Parpola, 2020; Yang, 2018). Intriguingly, Indus Valley cowries are not from the species *Monetaria moneta*, although they still likely come from the Indian Ocean (Parpola, 2020: 187). Cowries have also been found at the Neolithic site of Burzahom in the Karakoram Mountains, indicating their long-distance trade starting from at least the third millennium BCE (Miller, 2016). Yang (2018: 44) suggests that the poor documentation of cowrie-shell finds from early India might be due to their association in modern times with "small" money (used for minor transactions between nonelites), which has posed a challenge to the comprehensive study of archaeological finds. Hopefully, future archaeological work will fill in gaps regarding the earliest history of cowrie-shell use in India.

Many scholars assume that cowries were used as money in India from the Mauran period (321–185 BCE) and onward, but evidence of cowrie use during this period is limited (Heimann, 1980). The earliest clear evidence for cowries as money comes from travelers' accounts during the first millennium CE. The Chinese Buddhist pilgrim Faxian traveled to India in the early fifth century CE, and in his accounts of his travels he briefly mentions the use of cowries for exchange in Mathura, providing the first reference of shell money being used in India (Yang, 2018). From the seventh century and onward, many Chinese pilgrims to India recorded seeing cowries used as money, firmly establishing that shells were being used then alongside and together with metal coins. Chinese accounts are also corroborated by descriptions of travelers and traders from the Arab world during the seventh century and onward (Yang, 2018). It is almost certain that cowries started to be used as money in the centuries prior to these written descriptions, but the exact origin is unfortunately difficult to determine. During the periods for which we have good evidence, cowries were used for a range of economic activities including market exchanges for all goods imaginable as well as the payment of taxes, fees, and debts (Heimann, 1980).

During modern times, cowries, metal coins, and other forms of money circulated side by side in India, and it is likely that these money systems originated in ancient India in tandem with each other (Heimann, 1980; Yang, 2018). Metal coins struck in gold, silver, and copper were used for major transactions, but a dearth of metals and low liquidity meant that these coins were too rare and too valuable to be used for most daily affairs. In early modern times, for example, the whole wealth of a village was often worth less than one rupee, making metal currencies impractical outside of elite circles (Bowrey, 1905: 199). Cowries filled the need for a low-value medium of exchange that could be used to purchase daily goods and to pay land taxes to village chiefs in smaller settlements (Heimann, 1980: 56). This created a dual currency system in which cowries were "small money" for ordinary exchanges, while metal coins circulated for high-value transactions. Using Graeber's test for money as a medium for daily transactions (see Section 1), cowries in ancient India might have been more "money-like" than metal coinage, which would have circulated primarily among economic elites.

At some point during the first millennium CE, the monetary use of cowries spread from India to Southeast Asia (Yang, 2018). As in India, there is a dearth of archaeological finds of cowries from the earliest periods of their use, forcing us to look to historical texts to establish when they were first used as money. Texts from ancient Thailand dating to the early second millennium show that cowrie shells were being used as a unit of value for large exchanges and that vast numbers were being raised in order to fund temples, pay debts, and purchase lands (Griswold & na Nagara, 1969; Yang, 2018). By the time of Marco Polo (and likely much earlier), cowries were being used for regular transactions in the Kingdom of Pegu in modern-day Myanmar (Yang, 2018; Yule, 2010). By 1511, Portuguese explorer Tomé Pires noted that in Pegu one could purchase a chicken for between 400 and 500 cowries, specifically mentioning the Maldives as their source (Cortesao, 2018: 100). Throughout this region, cowries were counted and denominated in sets of four (and often eighty as a multiple of four), pointing to the shared origin of the monetary cowrie system (Yang, 2018: 105). The widespread use of cowries in Southeast Asia indicates the strength of their appeal as a currency and the global reach of their use.

Cowries continued to be used in Bengal through the early twentieth century, although their use declined considerably throughout the nineteenth century (Garg, 2007; Yang, 2018). During the colonial period, the British East India Company originally tolerated the use of cowries, as they were able to profit from their importation from the Maldives (Garg, 2007). Instability caused by price fluctuations coupled with the difficulties involved in storing and counting vast sums of shells, however, eventually turned colonial officials against the cowrie (Garg, 2007). Over the course of the nineteenth century, cowries were gradually replaced by copper coins, whose value proved easier for British officials to control and manipulate. As discussed by Yang (2018: 61), one of the ultimate reasons behind the decline of the cowrie in India was the cessation of the Atlantic slave trade. High demand for cowries in West Africa had kept inflation in check in India through the removal of millions of shells from the subcontinent in the hulls of European ships bound for Africa. When European nations began to outlaw slavery in the early nineteenth century, the value of the cowrie rapidly plummeted. Such rapid inflation upended the cowries function as a store of value and signaled the end of its use as money in India.

4.4 Africa

The cowrie-money world had its origin in Asia and the Indian Ocean but reached its most widespread and modern extent in West Africa. Cowrie shells were used as currency in West Africa from the thirteenth century through to modern times and left a strong impression on the cultural history of the region (Green, 2019; Hogendorn & Johnson, 1986; Yang, 2018). In Ghana, the Akan word for cowrie (*sedee*) gives its name to the modern currency, the cedi (Green, 2019). The 200-cedi coin bore the image of a cowrie shell between 1967 and 2007 (Figure 19). In historical times, cowries were important religious objects and can be found adorning many West African art objects and ritual items from the nineteenth century. Cowries continue to hold symbolic importance in modern times and feature prominently in art, fashion, and graphic design in both Africa and diasporic communities throughout the world (Green, 2019). In the 2020 visual album *Black is King*, for example, the singer Beyoncé wore a headdress made from cowries (Knowles-Carter, 2020).

Figure 19 200-cedi coin from Ghana. Photo by Ahanta. From Wikimedia Commons. Used under Creative Commons Attribution-Share Alike 3.0 License

Other examples of the use of cowries abound in contemporary media and symbolically reference connections to African culture as well as themes of wealth and power.

The use of shells and shell beads in Africa has a long history that stretches back to Paleolithic times (see Section 1). Cowries from the Indian Ocean were traded to Egypt for jewelry as early as the Bronze Age (Hogendorn & Johnson, 1986: 15). By medieval times, large amounts of cowries were being shipped from the Maldives to ports in Egypt and Yemen, from which they reached destinations across the Mediterranean world (Hogendorn & Johnson, 1986; Yang, 2018). The first Indian Ocean cowries likely reached West Africa via caravan routes from northern Africa and Egypt during the eleventh century (Figure 20) (Hogendorn & Johnson, 1986). Long-distance trade in Indian glass beads to southern Africa had likely followed similar routes several centuries earlier, linking the two regions by the seventh century at the latest (Klehm, 2021; Klehm & Dussubieux, 2022). By the fourteenth century, numerous accounts from travelers and traders indicate that cowries imported from the Maldives were in use as money in the Mali Empire and other regions of West Africa (Curtin, 1983; Green, 2019; Hogendorn & Johnson, 1986; Yang, 2018).

The cowrie shell was not the first type of money to be used in West Africa. Many other commodities, including gold, silver, copper, iron, and cloth, were

Figure 20 Painting by R. K. Thomas showing Arab traders conducting business with cowrie money. Painted in 1845. Public domain image from Wikimedia Commons

used as exchange media and stores of value at different points of time in West African history (Green, 2019; Hogendorn & Johnson, 1986). Curtin (1983: 252–253) suggests that the money cowrie replaced previously circulating Indigenous shell monies (including *Olivella* shells). With the value of the cowrie being higher than local shells due to the long-distance trade routes required to supply them, Curtin suggests that cowries rapidly replaced these earlier shell monies and became the only form of shell currency in circulation. Standardized ostrich-shell beads were also widely circulated in southern Africa from very early times, although it is unclear if these beads worked as money (Klehm, 2021). Hopefully, future archaeological work will help determine the antiquity of shell-money use in ancient Africa.

The history of the cowrie shell in Africa was forever transformed by European trade in African slaves starting in the sixteenth century (Green, 2019; Hogendorn & Johnson, 1986). Portuguese traders active in the Indian Ocean during the early 1500s made note of the vast quantities of cowries being produced on the Maldives for use in India and Southeast Asia and realized that these shells might have value in Africa. Soon thereafter, Portuguese traders in Asia started filling their hulls with cowries as ballast when shipping goods from India to European markets. Once in Europe, these ships would exchange their Asian goods for European ones bound for Africa, where they would arrive with a hull literally filled with money. Soon other European nations began to fill ships bound for Africa with cowries from the Maldives, with the rate of transport drastically increasing with the rapid growth of the Atlantic slave trade to North America and the Caribbean during the seventeenth and eighteenth centuries. (Yang, 2018). On the coasts of West Africa, European slavers often found that cowries were the means of payment most preferred by their local trading partners (Green, 2019; Hogendorn & Johnson, 1986; Yang, 2018). During the eighteenth century alone, over 26 million cowries are documented as having been shipped from the Indian Ocean to West Africa (Yang, 2018: 176).

Importing millions of cowries by sea in the hulls of European ships caused the rapid devaluation of the cowrie in West Africa. Over the course of the eighteenth century, the cowrie depreciated in value by some 75 percent (Yang, 2018: 175–176). Despite fluctuation in value, the cowrie cemented its hold as a currency in West Africa during this time and became an official currency in several West African states, including the powerful Dahomey Kingdom in modern-day Benin (Green, 2019; Hogendorn & Johnson, 1986; Polanyi, 1969; Yang, 2018). The abolition of the slave trade in the early 1800s led to a rapid decline in the importation of cowries. The value of the cowrie stabilized, however, after they started to be used by European traders to purchase palm oil, which was exported from West Africa in massive quantities during the second half of the nineteenth century (Yang, 2018). In the late nineteenth century, a new species of cowrie, *Cypraea annulus*, started to be imported to West Africa overland from the east coast of the African continent by German and French traders seeking to compete with the Dutch- and English-dominated trade from the Maldives (Yang, 2018). During the late nineteenth and early twentieth centuries, both species of cowries continued to circulate as "small money," coexisting with metal coins issued by colonial powers (Green, 2019; Yang, 2018). Several colonial governments attempted to prohibit the use of cowries as money in favor of national currencies, but results were mixed, with cowries still being used for small transactions into the middle of the twentieth century.

The story of the cowrie shell in Africa shows the broad reach of shell money. From their origins in the Maldives, cowries were traded to the far corners of China and Africa, becoming one of the world's first global currencies. As was the case with Chumash shell beads in the interior of North America, the value of cowrie shells from the Maldives was largely derived from the length of the trade networks that supplied them to different world regions. Circulating as currency thousands of kilometers from their point of origin, cowries were difficult to counterfeit and maintained a steady value until new forms of shipping and transportation disrupted their supply chains. Compared to the other examples in this Element, cowries represent a case study of shell money that was often accepted and promoted by states and governments. Their early use, however, still seems to have come from their movement through long-distance networks and use as an exchange medium across borders. Cowries also proved highly difficult for states to control, as evidenced by the very gradual decline in the use of cowries in modern India and Africa. Used for thousands of years across several continents and in a multitude of different economic and cultural systems, cowries show that shell money has been one of the longest lasting and most versatile social inventions in human history.

5 Conclusions and Future Directions

> *In every society that has preceded those in which gold, bronze, and silver have been minted as money, there have been other things, stones, shells, and precious metals in particular, that have been used and have served as a means of exchange and payment ... these precious objects have the same function as money in our societies and consequently deserve at least to be placed in the same category.*
>
> Mauss 1925 (2002), chapter 2, note 29

In the first section of this Element, I introduced money as a form of social technology that expands the economic possibilities of the societies that invent, adopt, and use it. By taking this approach, I suggested that we move away from "one size fits all" definitions that hold all forms of money up to the modern

Western model for strict comparison. Instead, I suggested that we see money as a continuum, with different types of transferable money-objects operating in variable roles in the societies that use them. In examples throughout this Element, I detailed several case studies where shells and shell beads functioned in similar ways to modern money and others where their use was dissimilar. In all cases, shell money was critical to the functioning of local and regional economies, allowing for economic formulations and opportunities that would have been impossible without its use.

Treating money as a continuum does not mean that we should abandon traditional Western definitions of money. On the contrary, the characteristics of money as a medium of exchange, a measure of value, a standard of deferred payment, and a store of value provide useful starting points from which to evaluate the monetary qualities of circulating objects. Just as modern money can take on and emphasize different functions in different contexts, however, we should not expect ancient money to fulfill all these roles in all situations. Ancient economies had substantial differences from ours today and adopted different money uses to accommodate their various needs. Money could function as both a social and a financial system of accounting, with different uses emphasized to varying degrees in different situations and societies. By describing the ways in which ancient commodities fulfilled standard characteristics of money to different extents, we can begin to understand how the money-like use of goods shaped the development of economic systems across human history. By comparing examples throughout this Element, I have sought to describe what shell money did for the societies that used it and outline the situations and conditions in which money came about.

The case studies in this Element follow a continuum from shells and shell beads functioning very differently from modern money to those that closely match all of money's standard functions. Cave finds from the Mediterranean show that shell beads were being produced, used, and possibly traded as early as 115,000 years ago. Although these early beads were almost certainly not used as money, they show the antiquity of human interest in portable shells for decoration and adornment. During the Neolithic, *Spondylus* shells from the Mediterranean were traded far and wide across Europe, becoming one of the continent's first long-distance trade goods. Although these shells were markers of wealth and likely functioned as a medium of exchange, it is difficult to determine the degree to which they worked as money due to a lack of standardization and a lack of knowledge as to how exactly they were used. Ethnographic data from the Pacific gives us much more information regarding the use of shell necklaces and armbands traded as part of the Kula ring in the South Pacific. Although anthropologists differ as to whether or not these shells can be counted as money, they were often used to exchange for daily goods and subsistence items and have been described as money both by ethnographers and local people (Macintyre, 1983a).

More clear-cut examples of shell beads being used for money come from North America, Africa, and Asia. Shell beads were undoubtedly used as money in ancient and historical North America, where a wide range of different types of shell beads were traded and exchanged for economic purposes across vast parts of the continent's coastal and interior regions. *Olivella* shells from the Santa Barbara region of southern California were among the most intensely traded of these shell monies and were well documented by early Spanish travelers as having been used by all levels of society to pay debts, finance events, store wealth, and purchase daily goods. On the east coast, wampum was also widely traded and played a central role in Wendat and Iroquoian political economies. Cowrie shells from the Maldives also have a long history of use as money, being used for some of the first monetary systems in ancient China and being closely integrated into historical monetary economies in India and Africa. By the early modern period, European merchants and colonizers were also using shell beads as money, acquiring millions of them in the Maldives and shipping them across the world.

One of the most striking parallels between these case studies is the use of shell money as a medium of exchange in extensive trade systems that cross multiple political borders and cultural boundaries. From Neolithic Europe to pre-Columbian North America, shells and shell beads seem to have been one of the most widely traded goods in ancient history. A major reason for this is likely the physical nature of shells themselves, being small, durable, and easily transportable. Many of these exchange networks occurred in areas removed from the sources for shell-bead collection and manufacture. This allowed shell beads to maintain value, as they had to be acquired through trade. In other cases, value was created and maintained through the specialized labor required to drill and polish manufactured beads. In using shells to facilitate exchange, ancient traders greatly increased their capacity for commerce, expanding economic networks across economic and political boundaries. Shell beads were thus a critical social technology that linked parts of Africa, Asia, and vast regions of North America into interconnected commercial and cultural worlds (Smith & Fauvelle, 2015; Yang, 2018; Zappia, 2014).

Where, when, and why did shell beads become money? The answer seems to be tied to their role as a medium of exchange in long-distance trade networks. In many cases, such as Shang China, interior North America, and in the American Northeast, shells take on their most money-like characteristics in times of intense and increasing interaction between or within cultures and cultural regions. Interactions across different environmental and resource boundaries also promoted the development of shell money, as was the case with Trobriand islanders exchanging goods between different islands or ancient Californians trading between resource regions on the islands, mainland coast, and interior mountains. As these case studies show, money has developed in multiple times and places throughout history and can be seen as a testament to the economic creativity and problem-solving capacity of our species. While there were many pathways to the use of shell money, the parallels between these case studies indicate that it could be productive to search for other forms of money-objects or money-like systems in similar situations of intensive long-distance exchange and interregional interaction.

How can we identify the use of money in the past? In order to expand the economic capacity of a social group, money needs to be well distributed within that society. This means that we should find money present across different cross sections of society and also in areas where high amounts of economic activities take place, be they marketplaces, house groups, council houses, or other important economic structures. If money was being used in a regional interaction network, we should also expect to find it distributed in a wide geographic area that spans social boundaries. Distribution should thus be widespread both within a social group and across a geographical region. It is notable that unlike some forms of commodity money, shells have little use-value other than their role as an item of adornment. In this sense, they are more similar to precious metals such as gold and silver than more utilitarian commodity currencies such as iron ingots, salt, or, in modern times, cigarettes and alcohol. Nonetheless, to be considered as money, shells should not only be used as jewelry but must also fulfill some other social functions. This suggests that they would be found in a range of contexts including burials, hoards, caches, and household areas.

Standardization is another key physical characteristic of money. Without standardization, it is difficult for shell money to function as a unit of account, as values would vary between shells. Although some money-like shell-exchange systems, such as Kula exchange on the Trobriands, are famously unstandardized, most of the examples of shell money-objects discussed in this Element are either naturally standardized or polished and ground into highly uniform beads. Standardization and distribution are the two characteristics of shell money that are the most likely to be identified in the archaeological record. For manufactured shell money such as beads, other factors such as the labor involved in production and the elaboration of the final product are also important considerations (Gamble, 2020). Archaeologists interested in identifying the origins of money-like exchange systems in the past should look for highly standardized and well-dispersed objects that appear in correlation with periods of marked growth in economic activity and elaboration.

Several of the case studies in this Element have described the use of money in nonstate societies. This includes well-documented cases such as in southern California, where shell beads circulating in hunter-gatherer societies fully conformed to modern definitions of money. These examples show that the use of money preceded state formation and illustrate a long human history of experimentation with money-like economic systems. This does not mean that there is no connection between state formation and the use of money. Scholars have documented how money is effective for state activities such as the collection of taxes, the financing of warfare, and the functioning of bureaucratic institutions (Graeber, 2011; Scott, 2017; Rosenswig, 2023). This means that early states often develop and spread monetary systems. Even if the origins of money were independent of the state, the fact that money is now used in all corners of the globe is likely due to the emergence and dominance of states as a social institution.

While the origins of money predate the state, the use of money was likely one of many factors that facilitated early state formation. In this Element, I argue that money develops as a social technology to solve a problem involving exchanges across boundaries and between strangers. In so doing, money likely opened up possibilities and problems that were never anticipated by its first users. The ability to store value in the form of shells and other money-objects also allowed individuals and groups the capacity to accumulate wealth on a far greater level than before. This would have facilitated the formation of systems of entrenched inequality. In southern California, for example, the formation of Chumash chiefdoms followed in the millennia after the invention and adaptation of shell-bead money. The presence of money would also have paved the way for the formation of early states by providing a ready means for states to collect taxes and finance their activities. An example of this process can be seen in the case of colonial New England, where expanding European states found utility in the use of wampum shell beads. The development of money, therefore, may have been one of several processes that inadvertently paved the way to the formation and spread of state systems throughout the world. Studying the connection between the use of early money and the origins of the state is a promising subject for future research.

Another important area for future studies of shell money is the connection between ancient globalizations and the invention of money. Many of the examples of shell money discussed in this Element come from periods of considerable regional integration and interaction. Cowries, for example, were a global money in the fullest sense of the word, with shells collected on the

Maldives shipped across several oceans and used on two continents (Yang, 2018). Other examples also circulated widely within shared global cultures that can qualify as ancient episodes of globalization (Jennings, 2011). *Olivella* shell money from Pacific California circulated throughout a vast Indigenous interior known world characterized by intensive communication and interaction (Smith & Fauvelle, 2015; Zappia, 2014). *Spondylus* shells in Neolithic Europe were also exchanged in the context of a cultural moment that included the spread of the Linear Pottery culture and associated process of neolithicization (Windler, 2019). Studying how money was shaped by and helped facilitate widespread interaction can help us understand these important periods of ancient integration and interaction.

This Element focuses on shell money because it was one of the most widespread and commonly used forms of nonmetal money in the ancient world. Many other goods and commodities, however, have been used as money by different societies throughout history. Examples include salt, cacao, textiles, feathers, stone beads, iron bars, and many others (Baron & Millhauser, 2021; Baron, 2018; Grossman & Paulette, 2020; Houston, 2012; McKillop, 2021). Many examples represent independent developments of money, while others were used in the context of previously existing monetary economies. Understanding the different contexts in which money has developed at various times and places is another important goal for future archaeological and anthropological work on ancient and premodern economies.

The case studies of shell money discussed in the previous sections can help formulate comparative hypotheses regarding the origins of other types of money in prestate societies. First, money seems to develop in regions characterized by intense regional and cultural interaction, where a medium of exchange is needed to help facilitate trade across social boundaries. Resource patchiness plays a key role, as it encourages exchange while requiring a comparison of value between different types of goods. Second, durable, standardized, or otherwise fungible items are the most likely to be used as money. In order to control inflation, these items must be difficult to procure due to natural scarcity, elite control, or the labor needed to produce them. Money must also be removed from circulation either through external trade or regular destruction in burials or caches. Finally, we can expect that the adoption of money will in many circumstances lead to increases in degrees of political hierarchy. The study of money is important for archaeology, as its materiality and cultural importance makes it one of the best ways for us to examine the origins and transmission of early economic complexity (e.g. Earle, 2004). Hopefully, these hypotheses and the other case studies presented in this

Element will help archaeologists compare and examine the various routes, forms, and roles that money has taken across human history.

The examples presented in this Element have illustrated the wide range of both physical and social forms that money has taken over the course of human history. Money has been used as an exchange medium between strangers in wide-ranging trade networks and also as a unit of account and taxation in early states. It has developed at multiple times and places and has been used by hunters and gatherers, agriculturalists, and industrialists. The fact that money can exist without capitalism or the state should not fill us with dismay over money's tenacity but should instead give us hope for the great variety of human economic creativity. One of the gifts of archaeology is the ability to peer into our past and examine the multitude of political and economic formations that humans have experimented with (Graeber & Wengrow, 2021). This rich history shows that the economic and political world that we know today is only one of many different possibilities. By examining the diversity of forms that money has taken throughout our past, perhaps we can be inspired to imagine and innovate new economic systems for our future.

References

Alday, A. (1995). Los elementos de adorno personal de la cueva del Moro de Olvena y sus derivaciones cronológico-culturales. *Bolskan*, 193–214.

Álvarez Fernandez, E. (2010). Shell Beads of the Last Hunter-Gatherers and Earliest Farmers in South-Western Europe. *Munibe Antropologia-Arkeologia*, 61, 129–138.

Andersson, J. G. (1932). *Den gula jordens barn: Studier över det förhistoriska Kina*. Bonnier.

Arias, P. (2002). La cueva de los Canes (Asturias): Los últimos cazadores de la Península Ibérica ante la muerte. Trabajo de Investigación Presentado para el Concurso de Provisión de una Plaza de Catedrático de Universidad Universidad de Cantabria, Santander.

Arnold, J. E. (1992). Complex Hunter-Gatherer-Fishers of Prehistoric California: Chiefs, Specialists, and Maritime Adaptations of the Channel Islands. *American Antiquity*, 57(1), 60–84.

Arnold, J. E. (1995). Transportation Innovation and Social Complexity among Maritime Hunter Gatherer Societies. *American Anthropologist*, 97(4), 733–747.

Arnold, J. E. (2001). *The Origins of a Pacific Coast Chiefdom: The Chumash of the Channel Islands*. University of Utah Press.

Arnold, J. E. (2012). Prestige Trade in the Santa Barbara Channel Region. *California Archaeology*, 4(1), 145–148.

Arnold, J. E., & Graesch, A. P. (2001). The Evolution of Specialized Shellworking among the Island Chumash. In J. E. Arnold (ed.), *The Origins of a Pacific Coast Chiefdom: The Chumash of the Channel Islands*, pp. 71–112. University of Utah Press.

Arnold, J. E., & Graesch, A. P. (2004). The Later Evolution of the Island Chumash. In J. E. Arnold (ed.), *Foundations of Chumash Complexity*, pp. 1–16. Cotsen Institute of Archaeology.

Arnold, J. E., & Martin, L. S. (2014). Botanical Evidence of Paleodietary and Environmental Change: Drought on the Channel Islands, California. *American Antiquity*, 79(2), 227–248.

Arnold, J. E., & Munns, A. (1994). Independent or Attached Specialization: The Organization of Shell Bead Production in California. *Journal of Field Archaeology*, 21(4), 473–489.

Arnold, J. E., & Rachal, D. (2002). The Value of Pismo Clam Tube Beads in California: Experiments in Drilling. *North American Archaeologist*, 23(3), 187–207.

Austen, L. (1945). Cultural Changes in Kiriwina. *Oceania*, 16(1), 15–60.

Bandelier, A. F. (1890). Contributions to the History of the Southwestern Portion of the United States. *Papers of the Archaeological Institute of America, America Series* 5.

Barbier, B. (2019). What a Bead Costs: An Experimental Approach to Quantifying Labor Investment in *Olivella* Bead Production. *Journal of California and Great Basin Anthropology*, 39(2), 145–159.

Baron, J., & Millhauser, J. (2021). A Place for Archaeology in the Study of Money, Finance, and Debt. *Journal of Anthropological Archaeology*, 62, 101278. https://doi.org/10.1016/j.jaa.2021.101278.

Baron, J. P. (2018). Making Money in Mesoamerica: Currency Production and Procurement in the Classic Maya Financial System. *Economic Anthropology*, 5(2), 210–223.

Beaglehole, E. (1937). Notes on Hopi Economic Life. *Yale University Publications in Anthropology*, 15.

Begg, D., Vernasca, G., Fischer, S., & Dornbusch, R. (2014). *Economics*. McGraw Hill.

Benito, J. L. P. (2005). Los talleres de cuentas de Cardium en el Neolítico peninsular. *Actas del III Congreso del Neolítico en la Península Ibérica: Santander, 5 a 8 de Octubre de 2003*, 277–286.

Bennyhoff, J. A., & Hughes, R. E. (1987). *Shell Bead and Ornament Exchange Networks between California and the Western Great Basin: Anthropological Papers*, vol. 64. The American Museum of Natural History.

Birch, J., & Hart, J. P. (2018). Social Networks and Northern Iroquoian Confederacy Dynamics. *American Antiquity*, 83(1), 13–33.

Bissett, T. G., & Claassen, C. P. (2016). Portable X-ray Fluorescence in Sourcing Prehistoric Whelk Shell Artifacts: A Pilot Study from Eastern North America. *North American Archaeologist*, 37(3), 143–169.

Blackburn, T. C. (1975). *December's Child: A Book of Chumash Oral Narratives, Collected by JP Harrington*. University of California Press.

Blair, E. H. (2015). Glass Beads and Global Itineraries. In R. A. Joyce (ed.), *Things in Motion: Object Itineraries in Archaeological Practice*, pp. 81–99. SAR Press.

Bolton, H. E. (1908). *Spanish Exploration in the Southwest, 1542–1706*, vol. 18. Charles Scribner's Sons.

Bolton, H. E. (1930). *Font's Complete Diary of the Second Anza Expedition*, vol. 4. University of California Press.

Bourke, J. G. (1884). *The Snake-Dance of the Moquis of Arizona*. Charles Scribner's Sons.

Bouzouggar, A., Barton, N., Vanhaeren, M., et al. (2007). 82,000-Year-Old Shell Beads from North Africa and Implications for the Origins of Modern Human Behavior. *Proceedings of the National Academy of Sciences*, 104(24), 9964–9969.

Bowrey, T. (1905). *A Geographical Account of Countries round the Bay of Bengal, 1669 to 1679*. Hakluyt Society.

Bradley, J. W. (2011). Re-visiting Wampum and Other Seventeenth-Century Shell Games. *Archaeology of Eastern North America*, 39, 25–51.

Bray, F. (1999). Towards a Critical History of Non-Western Technology. In T. Brook and G. Blue (eds.), *China and Historical Capitalism: Genealogies of Sinological Knowledge*, pp. 158–209. Cambridge University Press.

Brown, K. M., Meyer, M., Hancock, E., Sandoval, N. I., & Farris, G. J. (2022). Status and Social Stratification at Mission La Purísima Concepción: An Intra-Site Investigation of Residential Space within the Chumash Rancheria'Amuwu. *International Journal of Historical Archaeology*, 27, 1–37.

Brück, J. (2015). Gifts or Commodities? Reconfiguring Bronze Age Exchange in Northwest Europe. In P. Suchowska-Ducke, S. Scott Reiter, & H. Vandkilde (eds.), *Forging Identities: The Mobility of Culture in Bronze Age Europe*, vol. 1, pp. 47–56. BAR International Series.

Brunton, R. (1975). Why Do the Trobriands Have Chiefs? *Man*, 10(4), 544–558. https://doi.org/10.2307/2800132.

Burns, G. R. (2019). Evolution of Shell Bead Money in Central California: An Isotopic Approach. PhD diss., University of California–Davis.

Campbell, S. F. (1983). Kula in Vakuta: The Mechanics of Keda. In J. W. Leach and E. Leach (eds.), *The Kula: New Perspectives on Massim Exchange*, pp. 201–227. Cambridge University Press.

Ceci, L. (1982). The Value of Wampum among the New York Iroquois: A Case Study in Artifact Analysis. *Journal of Anthropological Research*, 38(1), 97–107.

Clark, R. B. (1963). The Economics of Dentalium. *The Veliger*, 6, 9–19.

Cortesao, A. (2018). *The Suma Oriental of Tomé Pires: Volume I*. Taylor & Francis.

Crittenden, A. N., & Zes, D. A. (2015). Food Sharing among Hadza Hunter-Gatherer Children. *PLoS ONE*, 10(7), e0131996. https://doi.org/10.1371/journal.pone.0131996.

Curtin, P. D. (1983). Africa and the Wider Monetary World, 1250–1850. In J. F. Richards (ed.), *Precious Metals in the Later Medieval and Early Modern Worlds*, pp. 231–268. Carolina Academic Press.

D'Errico, F., Henshilwood, C., Vanhaeren, M., & van Niekerk, K. (2005). *Nassarius kraussianus* Shell Beads from Blombos Cave: Evidence for Symbolic Behaviour in the Middle Stone Age. *Journal of Human Evolution*, 48(1), 3–24. https://doi.org/10.1016/j.jhevol.2004.09.002.

D'Errico, F., & Vanhaeren, M. (2015). Upper Palaeolithic Mortuary Practices: Reflection of Ethnic Affiliation, Social Complexity, and Cultural Turnover. In C. Renfrew, I. Morley, & M. J. Boyd (eds.), *Death Rituals, Social Order and the Archaeology of Immortality in the Ancient World: "Death Shall Have No Dominion"*, pp. 45–62. Cambridge: Cambridge University Press. https://doi.org/10.1017/CBO9781316014509.005.

Dalton, G. (1965). Primitive Money. *American Anthropologist*, 67(1), 44–65.

Damon, F. H. (1978). Modes of Production and the Circulation of Value on the Other Side of the Kula Ring, Woodlark Island, Muyuw. PhD diss. Princeton University.

Diaz-Guardamino Uribe, M., Wheatley, D., Williams, E., & Garrido Cordero, J. (2016). *Los textiles elaborados con cuentas perforadas de Montelirio [The Montelirio Beaded Textiles]*. Junta de Andalucia.

Earle, D. D. (2005). The Mojave River and the Central Mojave Desert: Native Settlement, Travel, and Exchange in the Eighteenth and Nineteenth Centuries. *Journal of California and Great Basin Anthropology*, 25(1), 1–38.

Earle, T. (2004). Culture Matters in the Neolithic Transition and Emergence of Hierarchy in Thy, Denmark: Distinguished Lecture. *American Anthropologist*, 106(1), 111–125.

Earle, T. (2018). The Ecology and Politics of Primitive Valuables. In T. Earle (ed.), *Bronze Age Economics*, pp. 19–42. Routledge.

Fauvelle, M. (2011). Mobile Mounds: Asymmetrical Exchange and the Role of the Tomol in the Development of Chumash Complexity. *California Archaeology*, 3(2), 141–158.

Fauvelle, M. (2012). Myths of an Island Chiefdom: Super Chert and Golden Acorns. A Response to Arnold. *California Archaeology*, 4(1), 149–152.

Fauvelle, M. (2013). Evaluating Cross-Channel Exchange in the Santa Barbara Region: Experimental Data on Acorn Processing and Transport. *American Antiquity*, 78(4), 790–798.

Fauvelle, M. (2014). Acorns, Asphaltum, and Asymmetrical Exchange: Invisible Exports and the Political Economy of the Santa Barbara Channel. *American Antiquity*, 79(3), 573–575.

Fauvelle, M., Esch, E., & Somerville, A. (2017). Climate Change and Subsistence Exchange in Southern California: Was Western Sea-Purslane a Channel Island Trade Good? *American Antiquity*, 82(1), 183–188.

Fauvelle, M., & Perry, J. (2019). Material Conveyance and Trade in the Channel Region. In K. M. Gill, M. Fauvelle, & J. M. Erlandson (eds.), *An Archaeology of Abundance: Re-evaluating the Marginality of California's Islands*, pp. 191–225. University Press of Florida.

Fauvelle, M., & Perry, J. (2023). Fisher-Hunter-Gatherer Complexity on California's Channel Islands: Feasting, Ceremonialism, and the Ritual Economy. In C. P. Sampson (ed.), *Fisher-Hunter-Gatherer Complexity in North America*, pp. 194–224. University Press of Florida.

Fauvelle, M., & Somerville, A. D. (2021a). Spatial and Temporal Variation in Fisher-Hunter-Gatherer Diets in Southern California: Bayesian Modeling Using New Baseline Stable Isotope Values. *Quaternary International*, 601, 36–48.

Fauvelle, M., & Somerville, A. D. (2021b). Surf and Turf: A Dataset of Stable Isotope Values of Plants and Animals from Southern California. *Data in Brief*, 38, 107380.

Feinman, G. M., & Garraty, C. P. (2010). Preindustrial Markets and Marketing: Archaeological Perspectives. *Annual Review of Anthropology*, 39, 167–191.

Feinman, G. M., Lightfoot, K. G., & Upham, S. (2000). Political Hierarchies and Organizational Strategies in the Puebloan Southwest. *American Antiquity*, 65(3), 449–470. https://doi.org/10.2307/2694530.

Felten, S. (2022). *Money in the Dutch Republic: Everyday Practice and Circuits of Exchange*. Cambridge University Press.

Fenton, W. N. (1998). *The Great Law and the Longhouse: A Political History of the Iroquois Confederacy*. University of Oklahoma Press.

Figes, O. (2017). *A People's Tragedy: The Russian Revolution 1891–1924*. Random House.

Fitzgerald, R. T., Jones, T. L., & Schroth, A. (2005). Ancient Long-Distance Trade in Western North America: New AMS Radiocarbon Dates from Southern California. *Journal of Archaeological Science*, 32(3), 423–434.

Fitzpatrick, S., & Callaghan, R. (2008). Seafaring Simulations and the Origin of Prehistoric Settlers to Madagascar. In G. Clark, F. Leach, & S. O'Connor (eds.), *Islands of Inquiry: Colonisation, Seafaring and the Archaeology of Maritime Landscapes*. ANU Press. https://doi.org/10.22459/TA29.06.2008.03.

Frisbie, T. R. (1974). Hishi as Money in the Puebloan Southwest. In T. R. Frisbie (ed.), *Collected Papers in Honor of Florence Hawley Ellis*, pp. 120–142. Archaeological Society of New Mexico.

Gamble, L. H. (2002). Archaeological Evidence for the Origin of the Plank Canoe in North America. *American Antiquity*, 67(2), 301–315.

Gamble, L. H. (2008). *The Chumash World at European Contact: Power, Trade, and Feasting among Complex Hunter-Gatherers*. University of California Press.

Gamble, L. H. (2011). Structural Transformation and Innovation in Emergent Political Economies of Southern California. In K. E. Sassaman & D. H. J. Holly (eds.), *Hunter-Gatherer Archaeology as Historical Process*, pp. 227–248. University of Arizona Press.

Gamble, L. H. (2020). The Origin and Use of Shell Bead Money in California. *Journal of Anthropological Archaeology*, 60, 101237.

Gamble, L. H., Walker, P. L., & Russell, G. S. (2001). An Integrative Approach to Mortuary Analysis: Social and Symbolic Dimensions of Chumash Burial Practices. *American Antiquity*, 66(2), 185–212.

García Sanjuán, L., Vargas Jiménez, J. M., Cáceres Puro, L. M., et al. (2018). Assembling the Dead, Gathering the Living: Radiocarbon Dating and Bayesian Modelling for Copper Age Valencina de la Concepción (Seville, Spain). *Journal of World Prehistory*, 31, 179–313.

Garg, S. (2007). Non-metallic Currencies of India in Indian Ocean Trade and Economies. In H. R. Ray & E. A. Alpers (eds.), *Cross Currents and Community Networks: The History of the Indian Ocean World*, pp. 245–262. Oxford University Press.

Gill, K. M., Fauvelle, M., & Erlandson, J. M. (2019). *An Archaeology of Abundance: Reevaluating the Marginality of California's Islands*. University Press of Florida.

Goodwin, G. (1942). *The Social Organization of the Western Apache*. Chicago University Press.

Goody, J. (1977). *The Domestication of the Savage Mind*. Cambridge University Press.

Graeber, D. (1996). Beads and Money: Notes toward a Theory of Wealth and Power. *American Ethnologist*, 23(1), 4–24.

Graeber, D. (2001). *Toward an Anthropological Theory of Value: The False Coin of Our Own Dreams*. Palgrave Macmillan.

Graeber, D. (2011). *Debt: The First 5,000 Years*. Melville House.

Graeber, D. (2012). On Social Currencies and Human Economies: Some Notes on the Violence of Equivalence. *Social Anthropology/Anthropologie Sociale*, 20(4), 411–428.

Graeber, D., & Wengrow, D. (2021). *The Dawn of Everything: A New History of Humanity*. Penguin.

Green, T. (2019). *A Fistful of Shells: West Africa from the Rise of the Slave Trade to the Age of Revolution*. Penguin.

Gregory, C. A. (1982). *Gifts and Commodities*, Vol. 2. Academic Press.

Griswold, A. B., & na Nagara, P. (1969). The Asokarama Inscription of 1399 AD, Epigraphic and Historical Studies, No. 2. *Journal of the Siam Society*, 57(1), 29–56.

Grossman, K., & Paulette, T. (2020). Wealth-on-the-Hoof and the Low-Power State: Caprines as Capital in Early Mesopotamia. *Journal of Anthropological Archaeology*, 60, 101207.

Hamell, G. R. (1986). Life's Immortal Shell: Wampum among the Northern Iroquoians. Ms. in Possession of the Author (85 Pages).

Hardy, B. L., Moncel, M.-H., Kerfant, C., et al. (2020). Direct Evidence of Neanderthal Fibre Technology and Its Cognitive and Behavioral Implications. *Scientific Reports*, 10(1), Article 1. https://doi.org/10.1038/s41598-020-61839-w.

Heimann, J. (1980). Small Change and Ballast: Cowry Trade and Usage as an Example of Indian Ocean Economic History. *South Asia: Journal of South Asian Studies*, 3(1), 48–69.

Helms, M. W. (1993). *Craft and the Kingly Ideal: Art, Trade, and Power*. University of Texas Press.

Hoffmann, D., Angelucci, D., Villaverde, V., Zapata, J., & Zilhão, J. (2018). Symbolic Use of Marine Shells and Mineral Pigments by Iberian Neandertals 115,000 Years Ago. *Science Advances*, *2018*. https://doi.org/10.1126/sciadv.aar5255.

Hogendorn, J., & Johnson, M. (1986). *The Shell Money of the Slave Trade*. Cambridge University Press.

Houston, D. C. (2012). The Impact of Red Feather Currency on the Population of the Scarlet Honeyeater on Santa Cruz. In S. C. Tideman & A. Gosler (eds.), *Ethno-ornithology*, pp. 77–88. Routledge.

Hudson, T., Timbrook, J., & Rempe, M. (1978). *Tomol: Chumash Watercraft as Described in the Ethnographic Notes of John P. Harrington*. Ballena Press.

Humphrey, C. (1985). Barter and Economic Disintegration. *Man*, 20(1), 48–72.

Ingham, G. (1996). Money Is a Social Relation. *Review of Social Economy*, 54(4), 507–529.

Ingham, G. (2013). *The Nature of Money*. John Wiley & Sons.

Jacobs, W. R. (1949). Wampum: The Protocol of Indian Diplomacy. *The William and Mary Quarterly: A Magazine of Early American History*, 6(4), 596–604.

Jennings, J. (2011). *Globalizations and the Ancient World*. Cambridge University Press.

Jevons, W. S. (1875). *Money and the Mechanism of Exchange*. C. Kegan Paul and Co.

Johnson, J. R. (1988). *Chumash Social Organization: An Ethnohistoric Perspective*. University of California, Santa Barbara.

Kander, J., Ebb, F., & Masteroff, J. (1966). *Cabaret* [Broadway Musical].

Keesing, R. M. (1990). New Lessons from Old Shells: Changing Perspectives on the Kula. In J. Siikala (ed.), *Culture and History in the Pacific*, pp. 139–163. Helsinki University Press.

Kehoe, A. B. (2002). *America before the European Invasions*. Longman.

Kennett, D. J. (2005). *The Island Chumash: Behavioral Ecology of a Maritime Society*. University of California Press.

King, C. (1976). Chumash Inter-Village Economic Exchange. In L. J. Bean & T. C. Blackburn (eds.), *Native Californians: A Theoretical Retrospective*, pp. 289–318. Ballena Press.

King, C. (1990). Evolution of Chumash Society: A Comparative Study of Artifacts Used for Social System Maintenance in the Santa Barbara Channel Region before A.D. 1804. In *The Evolution of North American Indians*. Garland Publishing.

Klehm, C. (2021). Material Histories of African Beads: The Role of Personal Ornaments in Culture Change. In H. Mattson (ed.), *Personal Adornment and the Construction of Identity*, pp. 135–145. Oxbow.

Klehm, C., & Dussubieux, L. (2022). Chemical Analysis of Precolonial Indian Ocean Glass Beads Found in the Southern African Interior. In H. Walder & L. Dussubieux (eds.), *The Elemental Analysis of Glass Beads: Technology, Chronology and Exchange*, p. 305–322. Leuven University Press.

Knapp, G. F. (1924). *The State Theory of Money*. Macmillan.

Knowles-Carter, B. (director). (2020). *Black Is King*. Disney+.

Kozuch, L. (2002). Olivella Beads from Spiro and the Plains. *American Antiquity*, 67(4), 697–709.

Kozuch, L., Walker, K. J., & Marquardt, W. H. (2017). Lightning Whelk Natural History and a New Sourcing Method. *Southeastern Archaeology*, 36(3), 226–240.

Kroeber, A. L. (1976). *Handbook of the Indians of California*. General Publishing Company.

Latta, F. F. (1949). *Handbook of Yokuts Indians by FF Latta*. Bear State Books.

Li, M. (2018). *Social Memory and State Formation in Early China*. Cambridge University Press.

Litster, M. (2016). Cowry Shell Money and Monsoon Trade: The Maldives in Past Globalizations. PhD diss. Australian National University.

Macintyre, M. (1983a). *Changing Paths: An Historical Ethnography of the Traders of Tubetube*. Australian National University.

Macintyre, M. (1983b). *The Kula: A Bibliography*. CUP Archive.

Macintyre, M., & Young, M. (1982). The Persistence of Traditional Trade and Ceremonial Exchange in the Massim. *Melanesia: Beyond Diversity*, 1, 207–22.

Malinowski, B. (1921). The Primitive Economics of the Trobriand Islanders. *The Economic Journal*, 31(121), 1–16.

Malinowski, B. (1922). *Argonauts of the Western Pacific: An Account of Native Enterprise and Adventure in the Archipelagoes of Melanesian New Guinea*. Routledge.

Malinowski, B. (1935). *Coral Gardens and Their Magic: A Study of the Methods of Tilling the Soil and of Agricultural Rites in the Trobriand Islands. Vol. 2: The Language of Magic and Gardening*. American Book Company.

Mann, M. (1986). *The Sources of Social Power: Vol. 1: A History of Power from the Beginning to A.D. 1760*. Cambridge University Press.

Martin, F. (2013). *Money: The Unauthorised Biography*. Bodley Head.

Marx, K. (1859). A Contribution to the Critique of Political Economy. *Marx and Engels Collected Works*, 29. Verlag von Franz Dunder.

Mauss, M. (2002). *The Gift: The Form and Reason for Exchange in Archaic Societies*. Routledge.

McKillop, H. (2021). Salt as a Commodity or Money in the Classic Maya Economy. *Journal of Anthropological Archaeology*, 62, 101277.

Mikkelsen, E. (2000). *Archaeological Excavations of a Monastery at Kaasidhoo: Cowrie Shells and Their Buddhist Context in the Maldives*. National Centre for Linguistic and Historical Research.

Miller, H. J. (2016). Spiraling Interconnectedness: A Fresh Look at Double-Spiral-Headed Pins in the Indian Subcontinent. In S. A. Abraham, P. Gullapalli, T. P. Raczek, & U. Z. Rizvi (eds.), *Connections and Complexity: New Approaches to the Archaeology of South Asia*, pp. 223–238. Routledge.

Miller, J. M., & Wang, Y. V. (2021). Ostrich Eggshell Beads Reveal 50,000-Year-Old Social Network in Africa. *Nature*, 601, 234–239.

Milliken, R., Fitzgerald, R. T., Hylkema, M. G., et al. (2007). Punctuated Culture Change in the San Francisco Bay Area. In T. L. Jones & K. A. Klar (eds.), *California Prehistory: Colonization, Culture, and Complexity*, pp. 99–124. Altamira Press.

Müller, J. (1997). Neolithische und chalkolithische Spondylus-Artefakte: Anmerkungen zu Verbreitung, Tauschgebiet und sozialer Funktion. In C. Becker, M. L. Dunkelmann, C. Metzner-Nebelsick, et al. (eds.), *Chronos. Beiträge zur Prähistorischen Archäologie zwischen Nord- und Südosteuropa.*

Festschrift für Bernhard Hänsel, pp. 91–106. VML Vlg Marie Leidor. Espelkamp, Leidorf.

Nigra, B. T., & Arnold, J. E. (2013). Explaining the Monopoly in Shell-Bead Production on the Channel Islands: Drilling Experiments with Four Lithic Raw Materials. *Journal of Archaeological Science*, 40(10), 3647–3659.

Parpola, A. (2020). Iconographic Evidence of Mesopotamian Influence on Harappan Ideology and Its Survival in the Royal Rites of the Veda and Hinduism. In I. L. Finkel & S. J. Simpson (eds.), *Context: The Reade Festschrift*, pp. 183–190. Archaeopress.

Peña, E. (2003). Making "Money" the Old-Fashioned Way: Eighteenth-Century Wampum Production in Albany. In C. L. Fisher (ed.), *People, Places, and Material Things: Historical Archaeology of Albany, New York*, pp. 121–127. New York State Museum.

Peneder, M. (2022). Digitization and the Evolution of Money as a Social Technology of Account. *Journal of Evolutionary Economics*, 32(1), 175–203. https://doi.org/10.1007/s00191-021-00729-4.

Peng, K., & Zhu, Y. (1995). *New Research on the Origin of Cowries in Ancient China*. University of Pennsylvania.

Pfaffenberger, B. (1992). Social Anthropology of Technology. *Annual Review of Anthropology*, 21, 491–516.

Polanyi, K. (1969). *Dahomey and the Slave Trade: An Analysis of an Archaic Economy*. University of Washington Press.

Powell, H. A. (1960). Competitive Leadership in Trobriand Political Organization. *The Journal of the Royal Anthropological Institute of Great Britain and Ireland*, 90(1), 118–145.

Powell, M. (1996). Money in Mesopotamia. *Journal of the Economic and Social History of the Orient*, 39(3), 224–242.

Rahmstorf, L. (2016). From "Value Ascription" to Coinage: A Sketch of Monetary Developments in Western Eurasia from the Stone to the Iron Age. In C. Haselgrove & S. Krmnicek (eds.), *The Archaeology of Money: Proceedings of the Workshop "Archaeology of Money", University of Tübingen, October 2013*, pp. 19–42. Leicester Archaeology Monographs, School of Archaeology & Ancient History, University of Leicester.

Rosenswig, R. (2023). Money, Currency and Heterodox Macroeconomics for Archaeology. *Current Anthropology*, 64(6), *In Press*.

Schumpeter, J. A. (1917). Das Sozialprodukt und die Rechenpfennige. Glossen und Beitrage zur Geldtheorie von Heute, *Archiv fur Sozialwissenschaft und Sozialpolitik* 44, 627–715.

Scott, J. C. (2017). *Against the Grain: A Deep History of the Earliest States*. Yale University Press.

Séfériadès, M. L. (2010). Spondylus and Long-DistanceTrade in Prehistoric Europe. In D. W. Anthony & J. Chi (eds.), *The Lost World of Old Europe: The Danube Valley, 5000–3500 BC*, pp. 179–186. Princeton University Press.

Shell, M. (2013). *Wampum and the Origins of American Money.* University of Illinois Press.

Simpson, L. B. (1961). *Journal of Longinos Martínez: Notes and Observations of the Naturalist of the Botanical Expedition in Old and New California and the South Coast 1791–1792.* John Howell Books.

Smith, E., & Fauvelle, M. (2015). Regional Interactions between California and the Southwest: The Western Edge of the North American Continental System. *American Anthropologist*, 17(4), 710–721.

Smith, W. H. (2002). Trade in Molluskan Religiofauna between the Southwestern United States and Southern California. PhD. diss. University of Oregon.

Sprague, R. (2004). Incised Dentalium Shell Beads in the Plateau Culture Area. *BEADS: Journal of the Society of Bead Researchers*, 16(1), 51–68.

Srinivasan, D. M. (1983). Vedic Rudra-Śiva. *Journal of the American Oriental Society*, 103(3), 543–556.

Stevenson, B., & Wolfers, J. (2020). *Principles of Economics.* Worth Publishers.

Stibbard-Hawkes, D. N. E., Smith, K., & Apicella, C. L. (2022). Why Hunt? Why Gather? Why Share? Hadza Assessments of Foraging and Food-Sharing Motive. *Evolution and Human Behavior*, 43(3), 257–272. https://doi.org/10.1016/j.evolhumbehav.2022.03.001.

Szabó, K. (2018). Shell Money and Context in Western Island Melanesia. In A. Clark, L. Carreau, & E. Lilje (eds.), *Pacific Presences, Oceanic Art and European Museums*, vol. 2, pp. 25–38. Sidestone Press.

Thierry, F. (2018). Currency. In P. Goldin (ed.), *Routledge Handbook of Early Chinese History*, pp. 336–366. Routledge.

Trigger, B. G. (1987). *Children of Aataentsic: A History of the Huron People to 1660*, vol. 2. McGill-Queen's Press-MQUP.

Trinkaus, E., & Buzhilova, A. P. (2018). Diversity and Differential Disposal of the Dead at Sunghir. *Antiquity*, 92(361), 7–21. https://doi.org/10.15184/aqy.2017.223.

Tyner, J. A. (2020). "Currency Is a Most Poisonous Tool": State Capitalism, Nonmarket Socialism, and the Elimination of Money during the Cambodian Genocide. *Genocide Studies and Prevention*, 14(1), 143–158. https://doi.org/10.5038/1911-9933.14.1.1710.

Vandkilde, H. (2016). Bronzization: The Bronze Age as Pre-modern Globalization. *Praehistorische Zeitschrift*, 91(1), 103–123. https://doi.org/10.1515/pz-2016-0005.

Vanhaeren, M., d'Errico, F., Stringer, C., et al. (2006). Middle Paleolithic Shell Beads in Israel and Algeria. *Science*, 312(5781), 1785–1788. https://doi.org/10.1126/science.1128139.

Von Glahn, R. (1996). *Fountain of Fortune: Money and Monetary Policy in China, 1000–1700*. University of California Press.

Weiner, A. B. (1976). *Women of Value, Men of Renown: New Perspectives in Trobriand Exchange*. University of Texas Press.

Weld, W. (1963). Dentalium: The Money Shell of the Northwest Coast. *Washington Archaeologist*, 7(1), 4–18.

Whalen, M. (2013). Wealth, Status, Ritual, and Marine Shell at Casas Grandes, Chihuahua, Mexico. *American Antiquity*, 78(4), 624–639. https://doi.org/10.7183/0002-7316.78.4.624.

Windler, A. (2013). From the Aegean Sea to the Parisian Basin: How *Spondylus* Can Rearrange Our View on Trade and Exchange. *Metalla*, 20(2), 95–106.

Windler, A. (2019). The Use of *Spondylus gaederopus* during the Neolithic of Europe. *Journal of Open Archaeology Data*, 7. https://doi.org/10.5334/joad.59.

Woodward, A. (1934). An Early Account of the Chumash. *Masterkey*, 8(4), 118–123.

Yang, B. (2018). *Cowrie Shells and Cowrie Money: A Global History*. Routledge.

Yao, A. (2010). Recent Developments in the Archaeology of Southwestern China. *Journal of Archaeological Research*, 18, 203–239.

Yule, H. (ed.). (2010). *The Book of Ser Marco Polo, the Venetian: Concerning the Kingdoms and Marvels of the East*, trans. H. Yule, vol. 2. Cambridge University Press. https://doi.org/10.1017/CBO9780511702747.

Yung-Ti, L. (2003). On the Function of Cowries in Shang and Western Zhou China. *Journal of East Asian Archaeology*, 5(1–4), 1–26. https://doi.org/10.1163/156852303776172999.

Zappia, N. A. (2014). *Traders and Raiders: The Indigenous World of the Colorado Basin, 1540–1859*. University of North Carolina Press.

Zelizer, V. (2000). Fine Tuning the Zelizer View. *Economy and Society*, 29(3), 383–389. https://doi.org/10.1080/03085140050084570.

Zelizer, V. A. (2021). *The Social Meaning of Money: Pin Money, Paychecks, Poor Relief, and Other Currencies*. Princeton University Press.

Acknowledgements

I would like to thank Timothy Earle for encouraging me to write this Element and for providing helpful feedback on several early drafts. Many thanks also to Guillermo Algaze, Kaitlin Brown, and Peter Jordan for their thoughtful and constructive comments on various versions of the manuscript. I am also grateful to three anonymous reviewers who provided helpful comments and suggestions. I would also like to thank series editors Kenneth Hirth, Timothy Earle, and Emily Kate for inviting me to write this Element, for providing helpful comments on the manuscript, and for shepherding it through the editorial process. Thanks also to Robert Rosenswig for giving permission to cite his paper on ancient money that is currently in press. I am grateful to the Lund University Library and the Joint Faculties of Humanities and Theology at Lund University for covering the open access publishing fees for this Element. Finally, I would like to thank the many people in numerous institutions, conferences, and classrooms who have helped shape my thoughts on money, shell beads, and economic complexity. Any mistakes or omissions are of course my own.

Cambridge Elements ☰

Ancient and Pre-modern Economies

Kenneth G. Hirth

The Pennsylvania State University

Ken Hirth's research focuses on the development of ranked and state-level societies in the New World. He is interested in political economy and how forms of resource control lead to the development of structural inequalities. Topics of special interest include: exchange systems, craft production, settlement patterns, and preindustrial urbanism. Methodological interests include: lithic technology and use-wear, ceramics, and spatial analysis.

Timothy Earle

Northwestern University

Tim Earle is an economic anthropologist specializing in the archaeological studies of social inequality, leadership, and political economy in early chiefdoms and states. He has conducted field projects in Polynesia, Peru, Argentina, Denmark, and Hungary. Having studied the emergence of social complexity in three world regions, his work is comparative, searching for the causes of alternative pathways to centralized power.

Emily J. Kate

The University of Vienna

Emily Kate is bioarchaeologist with training in radiocarbon dating, isotopic studies, human osteology, and paleodemography. Having worked with projects from Latin America and Europe, her interests include the manner in which paleodietary trends can be used to assess shifts in social and political structure, the affect of migration on societies, and the refinement of regional chronologies through radiocarbon programs.

About the Series

Elements in Ancient and Premodern Economies is committed to critical scholarship on the comparative economies of traditional societies. Volumes either focus on case studies of well documented societies, providing information on domestic and institutional economies, or provide comparative analyses of topical issues related to economic function. Each Element adopts an innovative and interdisciplinary view of culture and economy, offering authoritative discussions of how societies survived and thrived throughout human history.

Cambridge Elements ᐧ

Ancient and Pre-modern Economies

Elements in the Series

Printed in the United States
by Baker & Taylor Publisher Services